HARLEY-DAVIDSON
KNUCKLEHEAD
EIGHTY YEARS

GREG FIELD

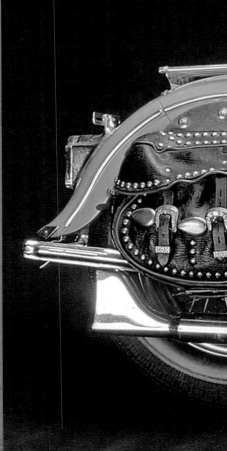

CRESTLINE

Brimming with creative inspiration, how-to projects, and useful information to enrich your everyday life, Quarto Knows is a favorite destination for those pursuing their interests and passions. Visit our site and dig deeper with our books into your area of interest: Quarto Creates, Quarto Cooks, Quarto Homes, Quarto Lives, Quarto Drives, Quarto Explores, Quarto Gifts, or Quarto Kids.

© 2016 Quarto Publishing Group USA Inc.
Text © 2016 Greg Field
Photography © Greg Field unless labeled otherwise.

This edition published in 2019 by Crestline,
an imprint of The Quarto Group
142 West 36th Street, 4th Floor
New York, NY 10018 USA
T (212) 779-4972 F (212) 779-6058
www.QuartoKnows.com

First published in 2016 by Motorbooks, an imprint of The Quarto Group, 100 Cummings Center, Suite 265-D, Beverly, MA 01915, USA.

Crestline titles are also available at discount for retail, wholesale, promotional, and bulk purchase. For details, contact the Special Sales Manager by email at specialsales@quarto.com or by mail at The Quarto Group, Attn: Special Sales Manager, 100 Cummings Center Suite 265D, Beverly, MA 01915, USA.

10 9 8 7 6 5 4 3 2 1

ISBN: 978-0-7858-3745-9

Acquiring Editor: Darwin Holmstrom
Project Manager: Jordan Wiklund
Creative Director: Laura Drew
Art Director: Brad Springer
Cover Designer: John Sticha
Book Designer: John Barnett
Layout: Rebecca Pagel

Front cover: 1947 Model EL. *David Blattel*
Back cover: 1937 Model EL.
Endpapers: 1936 EL Special Sport Solo model (front); 1947 Model EL (rear). *David Blattel*
Frontis: The Knucklehead engine, with its massive rocker covers, is considered a classic design among motorcycle enthusiasts everywhere.
Title page: Indicative of an early customized Harley, this 1947 FL sports many features not found on a stock model.

Printed in China

CONTENTS

ACKNOWLEDGMENTS

Without the help and encouragement of dozens of individuals, this book would still be just a bunch of disjointed ramblings on my computer's hard drive, so I offer my thanks to the following people.

First, to the foremost scholars of the 1936 Knucklehead, experts who were so helpful in my quixotic journey tabulating the zillion-and-one changes made to the Knucklehead that first year. Because of the effort of these men, Chapter 1 of the Knucklehead saga is much more complete: Jerry Hatfield, Chris Haynes, Casey Hoekstra, Doug Leikala, Gerry Lyons, and Herbert Wagner.

For letting me photograph their fine Knuckleheads: Dave Banks, Carman Brown, Eldon Brown, Rob Carlson, and Gary Strom; Jeff Coffman of Jeff's American Classics (Dundee, Oregon); the late Dave DeMartini of Northwest Custom Cycle (Snoqualmie, Washington); Valentino "Vic" Domowicz, Elmer Ehnes, Larry Engesether, Farmer Fred, Mike Golembiewski, Ron Lacey, Dave Monahan, Adolph Ogar, Wayne Pierce Sr., and Wayne Pierce Jr. of Pierce's Harley-Davidson in DeKalb, Illinois.

For sharing their knowledge, time, and photographs, or for helping me to find motorcycles to photograph: Rick Connor, Peter Egan, and George "Geo" Edwards of St. Paul Harley-Davidson (St. Paul, Minnesota); Brian Holden of the Deeley Motorcycle Museum (Vancouver, British Columbia); Rick "Chintzy" Krajewski of Competition Cycle (Milwaukee, Wisconsin); Dave Minerva, Gary Nelson, Bruce Palmer, Jerry Renner, and Steve Schlessinger at Jerry's House of Harley (Milwaukee, Wisconsin); Scott Rowinski and Carmen Tom of Downtown Harley-Davidson (Seattle, Washington); Tom Samuelsen; and Herbert Wagner.

For their long-term encouragement and support, I want to thank my parents, Laurie and Larry, my brothers and sisters—Scot, Shawn, Dawn, and Heather—and my good friends Owen Herman, Tim Lien, Tom Samuelsen, John Scharf, and Joe Sova.

For putting me up and putting up with me while in Milwaukee: Annie and Heidi Golembiewski; Ray, Becky, and Nicole Karshna; and Jim, Tracy, and Lexie Olson.

Finally, to Jeni, who put up with so much obsessive behavior and gave up so much for me to finish this manuscript.

If I've forgotten anyone, I hope they will forgive the oversight.

1

THE LEGEND BEGINS

Histor isn't often made in a ballroom, but it was on November 25, 1935. After years of rumors and sporadic sightings, the assembled throng of Harley-Davidson dealers at the annual dealers' convention was treated to a vision of their future—the company's future. When the curtains parted, there stood parked on the

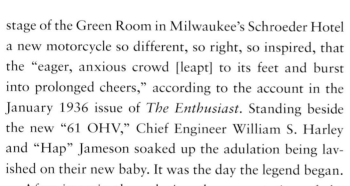

stage of the Green Room in Milwaukee's Schroeder Hotel a new motorcycle so different, so right, so inspired, that the "eager, anxious crowd [leapt] to its feet and burst into prolonged cheers," according to the account in the January 1936 issue of *The Enthusiast*. Standing beside the new "61 OHV," Chief Engineer William S. Harley and "Hap" Jameson soaked up the adulation being lavished on their new baby. It was the day the legend began.

After impatiently enduring the presentation of the whole 1936 lineup, the dealers rushed the stage to get a closer look at the new flagship of the line, Harley's new "little" Big Twin. The machine before them was a masterpiece from any angle, a bold fusion of art deco and streamlining that at once looked both fast and mannered. More importantly, it looked like a *motorcycle,* as if it had been created that way, not having slowly evolved from the first motorized bicycles that H-D had built. In fact, the only throwback to that heritage seemed to be the bicycle pedal on the kickstarter. The more the dealers looked, the more they appreciated.

Symmetry defined the new machine. Twin gas tanks straddled the frame's backbone tube, each with its own chrome-plated filler cap and petcock. Bridging the gap between the tanks was the new instrument panel featuring a large, integral, 100-mph speedometer (placed front and center, right where it would be easiest to read),

ABOVE: Not all 1930s riders were men. Margaret "Mugs" Pritchard of Appleton, Wisconsin, got her own 1932 Harley 45 model when she was just sixteen years old. *Herbert Wagner Collection*

OPPOSITE: Harley-Davidson opened a new chapter to its storied history when it launched the EL model in 1936. No doubt, this EL's wild colors drew a lot of attention! *Doug Mitchel*

an ammeter, an oil-pressure indicator, and the ignition switch. Twin downtubes swept down and back from the steering head to the rear axle clips. The sweeping V of the cylinders, highlighted on the right side by the gleaming pushrod covers, framed the dramatically slash-cut, chrome-plated air-intake horn. And those cylinders were topped by polished aluminum rocker housings, each with two-round, chrome-plated covers over the ends of the rocker shafts. It was everything the rumors had said—and everything the dealers had hoped it would be.

As far as the dealers were concerned, this was the Eighth Day, and creation was complete.

Enthusiasm for the new model spilled over to the banquet that evening. In fact, after soaking up copious amounts of the famous Milwaukee "suds," some of the dealers got a little out of control. During the turkey dinner, "two-gun 'Cactus Bill' Kennedy, a tough hombre from Phoenix, Arizona, [got] so excited . . . he [drew] a bead on the crystal chandelier, let out a blood-curdling yip-eee . . . and emptie[d] his six-gun . . . some of the more sedate dealers pass[ed] out . . . and the turkey on Bill's plate actually turn[ed] pale," according to *The Enthusiast*.

In the days that followed, the dealers toured the factory and attended sales seminars. History doesn't record whether H-D gave their dealers any further information on when the new model would be ready, but a curious thing happened after the curtain was drawn closed on the Green Room's stage: the most exciting new American motorcycle in over a decade disappeared completely, as if it had never been there at all. When Harley's 1936 models were announced to the public in the January 1936 issue of *The Enthusiast*, the new model—a machine that was truly innovative enough to warrant a good bit of hype— wasn't shown or mentioned at all. In fact, the only clue to its existence was a small photograph of the assembled dealers at the November convention: the new machine appears in the photo's background, so small that you'd have to know it was there to make it out. But the caption for the photo makes no mention of it, nor does the magazine's coverage of the convention. And so it would go, far into the machine's first year of production.

To the H-D Motor Company, its dealers' enthusiasm was welcome, but it also presented a quandary. Harley was eager to begin recouping its costs after more than four years of heavy spending to develop the OHV, but the company also knew what would happen if the new model was released before it was ready. Still smarting from the disastrous introduction of its last new Big Twin, the company decided on a more cautious approach this time.

ROOTS OF THE 61

The company's past had been built on the foundation of their early intake-over-exhaust, or F-head, engines that gave them such success from 1903 to 1929. The company's present was being built on the newer sidevalve, or flathead, engines that were introduced in 1929 (45-ci Series D) and 1930 (74-ci Series V), but these models proved disappointing in many ways. Initially, both were prone to trouble, especially the V series, which had so many problems that the production line was shut down to fix them after a flood of dealer complaints gave H-D no other choice. To their credit, H-D stood by its product, redesigning many parts to fix the problems on the production line and sending free kits to fix those bikes already on the streets. But the initial blunder had eroded confidence among the company's dealers and customers. They were wondering, was it an honest mistake, or was H-D inept and past its prime?

By 1931, most of the inadequacies of the first V-series machines had been fixed. Still, Harley's sidevalve models were somewhat disappointing because they weren't much better than the old F-heads they replaced. Worse yet, they suffered in performance compared to the equivalent Indian models. In short, the Harley side valves were decent motorcycles, but they weren't *exciting* motorcycles, certainly not exciting enough to win new customers, especially in hard times. Harley-Davidson needed something radically new on which to build its future.

The Great Depression

Motorcycle sales had been up and down for many years, but the trend was definitely down in 1931. In contrast, the trend had been up during the boom years of 1927–1929, when the side valves were introduced. In 1929, H-D sold 23,989 machines; this was the largest number sold since 1918, when sales of military bikes inflated annual sales to 26,708. Then came Black Thursday, October 24, 1929, which marked the first stock market collapse that kicked off the Great Depression. In a record bout of panic selling, 13 million shares were traded and prices plummeted. On the 29th, Black Tuesday, the real crash came. Stock prices went into a death spin, and 16 million shares were sold. In one week, $16 billion had evaporated.

Reverberations from the crash spread slowly across America in 1930. In the early part of the year, the stock market began to recover; those with wealth remained

One of H-D's more interesting classic machines was the model RLDR. Introduced in 1934 for Class C competition, this machine had racing parts in the engine but was otherwise fully street legal. The idea was that a guy could ride his bike to the race, take off the lights and front fender, and then compete on the racetrack. Afterwards he would put the road parts back on and then ride his bike home again. In 1937 the RLDR was superceded by the WLDR model with a fully circulating oiling system. This example, 36RLDR2232, was owned by Adolph Roemer of Milwaukee, shown here with his girlfriend, Ethel Sentenne. *Herbert Wagner Collection*

optimistic. Henry Ford, who had sold his one-millionth Model A the year before, opined that "These really are good times but only a few know it." Men of more modest means knew better, and they were not in a spending mood, especially for something as frivolous as a motorcycle.

Then came the final nail in the economic coffin. In June, Congress passed the Smoot-Hawley Act, which sharply raised tariffs. In retaliation, other countries raised theirs. Unemployment rose further, and H-D's export sales, which had been as much as 40 percent of the company's business during the 1920s, dropped off sharply. When the results were tallied at the end of the fiscal year,

H-D's overall sales for the year dropped by nearly 25 percent, to 18,036. The Great Depression had begun.

The Sump Oiler

Which brings us back to 1931, a desperate and historic year. Sales fell to 10,407, slightly more than half the number sold the previous year—and the lowest total since the 3,853 sold in 1912! Clearly, the company was in trouble. Salaries were cut, and hours had been slashed for nonsalaried workers.

Despite the gloom, William S. Harley never gave up. Instead, in a flash of inspiration worthy of the great Thomas Edison (who had died in October of that year,

The Model EL was the first production model to utilize an overhead-valve engine. To this day, all of Harley's Big Twin engines trace their DNA to that engine. *Doug Mitchel*

at age 84), he proposed developing the motorcycle that would ultimately save the company—an OHV twin with a recirculating oil system, known as the "sump oiler." The board of directors gave its approval, and work began on what would ultimately be the 61 OHV. And here's where our story really begins.

If 1931 was a year of hardship (and it was), 1932 was worse. The Dow dropped below 50. Over two million Americans wandered the country as vagrants. Unemployment rose to 24 percent overall, but it reached 50 percent in some cities. Along with it, the suicide rate rose 30 percent.

Hard times grew worse in Milwaukee, too. Harley-Davidson workers were laid off, and the company's four founders imposed on themselves a 50 percent pay cut. Production fell to 7,218, a reduction of 30 percent compared to the previous year. But a new source of income was in the offing. The board of directors was approached by their Japanese importer and the Sankyo industrial firm with an offer to purchase a license to manufacture H-D motorcycles in Japan—an offer that was ultimately accepted. As bad as things got, however, work continued on the OHV.

Things really bottomed out in Milwaukee in 1933. Harley sales fell by almost half again, to just 3,703 machines. But things also began looking up. Prototype parts for the new 61 were cast and assembled into working engines. Bench tests were promising, so the board agreed to continue development, scheduling the OHV to be their lead model for 1935. The board also approved the sale of a manufacturing license to the Sankyo firm in Japan. Sankyo began setting up to produce the H-D VL, under the trade name Rikuo.

The Depression slowly began to ease its grip on the economy in 1934. The Dow rose only slightly, but the gross national product (GNP) rose 17 percent (versus shrinking by 4 percent in 1933). Harley sales nearly tripled for 1934, to 11,212 units—aided by the late introduction of 1935 models, which occurred in December, rather than in September. Unfortunately, development of the 61 OHV had fallen behind schedule, so when the 1935 models were announced, the 61 OHV was not among them. The first rideable machine had been assembled and tested

in the spring and summer of 1934, but nagging problems with oil leaks prevented finalization of the design in time for 1935 production. The board of directors delayed introduction of the new model to 1936.

Recovery in the United States accelerated somewhat in 1935: the Dow rose to a high of 144, the GNP grew 9 percent, and unemployment fell to near 20 percent. In Milwaukee, H-D's OHV was nearing completion in the summer of 1935. According to board of directors minutes unearthed by noted motorcycle historian and author Jerry Hatfield and presented in his book *Inside Harley-Davidson*, there was even discussion of building two hundred 61s in the summer of 1935, but the sales department was opposed to the idea because they feared release of the 61 would adversely affect sales of the remaining 1935 side-valve Big Twins.

At the May meeting, the board discussed releasing the 61 in September 1935 or January 1936, even though continuing problems with chain and brake-lining wear caused some members of the board to suggest that the 61 project be scrapped altogether. Company president Walter Davidson suggested that a different combination of sprockets might reduce chain wear. Davidson's suggestions apparently resulted in changing the transmission sprocket from 19 teeth to 22 teeth and the rear sprocket from 45 teeth to 51 teeth (based on data in the book *1930 to 1949 Models: Operation, Maintenance, and Specifications*, published by Harley-Davidson), which resulted in enough of an improvement that the board resolved that they would "probably go ahead with the job" at their June meeting. Although it is not recorded in the minutes, continuing difficulties with the 61 may have resulted in the decision to push back the new model introduction into winter for the second year in a row.

Oil Control

The big problem that remained to be solved was control of oil to and from the rocker arms and valves. On the prototype 61s, the valves, valve springs, and rocker arms were left uncovered. Many other OHV machines of the day also had uncovered mechanisms, but the rockers on those machines were typically lubricated by grease that was periodically resupplied through a grease fitting. Not so on the 61 engine; its signature feature, the OHV system, was lubricated by oil bled off from the engine's other great new feature, its recirculating oil system. "Bled off" is a euphemism, since any lubricating oil supplied to lubricate the rockers, valves, and springs eventually ended up on the outside of the engine, and the slipstream quickly carried it back to splatter all over rider and machine.

Approval for Production

As summer turned to fall, the solution to the oiling problem remained elusive. Unfortunately, the introduction date for new models was fast approaching, and, having already delayed the 61 OHV's introduction by a year, the company's managers were loath to delay it any longer. At the October 1935 board meeting, the 61 was officially added to the lineup for 1936 and production was set for 1,600 units. No one knows whether approval came as a result of a long-sought solution to the oil control problem, or whether they made the decision with crossed fingers, trusting that luck and Bill Harley's design acumen would reveal a solution to the problem before full-scale production began. Evidence suggests the latter, because photographs developed as late as December show no evidence of valve spring enclosures on the 61.

Preproduction 61 OHVs

Consensus among many 1936 61 aficionados is that H-D built a dozen or so preproduction machines for continued testing, for presentation at the convention, and for photography. No records exist that tell how many were built or when they were built, but we can conclude a few things from existing photographs: at least two 61s were built with 1935 serial numbers; at least one of these was extensively road-tested; and the road-test machine leaked a lot of oil because it still lacked covers for the rockers and valves.

The first conclusion is based on photos that show the motorcycles with serial numbers 35E1002 and 35E1003. The second conclusion is supported by the engine-teardown photo of 35E1003, which shows the bike coated with grime and oil, its kickstarter pedal showing wear from use and damage from a light spill or tipover. The

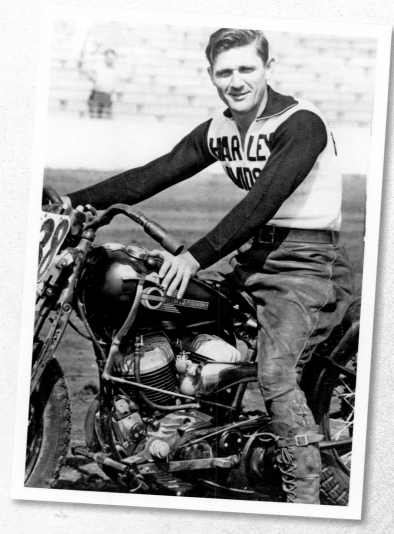

In 1941, competition star Tommy Hayes of Dallas, Texas, was voted the most popular rider in the USA. A few weeks earlier Hayes and another rider had been killed on the racetrack at Oakland, California. *Herbert Wagner Collection*

same photo supports the third conclusion, clearly showing that valve-spring covers were not used on these machines.

These photos also provide the only reliable time reference available to date the preproduction bikes. The photos of 35E1002 were processed on October 17, 1935. The photos of the oil-soaked 35E1003 were processed on November 14, 1935, described as "motor close-ups for Joe Ryan." (Joe Ryan was H-D's service manager at the time.) From this we can conclude that these preproduction machines had been completed no later than mid-October, more than a month before the 61's introduction at the convention.

The 61s serialed 35E1002 and 35E1003 are considered preproduction machines rather than experimental

The EL didn't earn its Knucklehead moniker until years later when it was replaced by the Panhead. Both names derive from the engines' respective rocker cover designs, one resembling knuckles, the other pans. *Doug Mitchel*

prototypes because their numbers are in the form of production serial numbers, rather than the form of experimental serial numbers (EX 3, for example). The serial numbers on these machines could also be taken as further proof that the 61 had been originally planned for the 1935 model line. The 61 OHV displayed at the November dealers' convention was likely one of these preproduction machines. Ultimately, these machines were probably scrapped.

Stealth Introduction

In the first dealer news bulletin following the dealers' convention—dated December 2, 1935—H-D issued its first printed words about the 61, to make it clear to all that the new model was not yet ready and that it might not be for some time:

> For several years rumors have been current all over the country about a new twin that H-D was developing and would have on the market any day. The most incredulous and many times positively amusing fabrications have been spread about this model. True, our engineering staff has been working for a long time on a model of new and original design and their efforts have finally reached the stage where such a motorcycle, a 61 cubic inch overhead, was shown to dealers in attendance at the National Dealers' Convention. However, production on this model will necessarily be extremely limited and we are therefore in no position to make a public announcement at this time. . . . Under no circumstances should this model be ordered as a demonstrator!

But, as we shall soon see, even as the company was admonishing their dealers not to order OHV demonstrators, the assembly line was being readied for production. Moreover, the new model had already been listed in a specification sheet, dated December 1, 1935, for standard and special equipment groups.

Pilot Production

Clearly, the company was still uneasy about the 61, despite dealer enthusiasm. One concerning issue was undoubtedly the lack of an effective means to return oil from the valve gear to the engine. Despite their

unease—according to Jerry Hatfield's *Inside Harley-Davidson*, based on the minutes of the December 16, 1935, board of directors meeting—company managers had earlier made the decision to press on, building "ten or fifteen" pilot production bikes by mid-December to "check the flow of parts through the various buildup levels."

The famous photo of the four company founders with what was reputed to be the first production 61 OHV was developed on December 12, 1935, showing the founders with one of the pilot production bikes. Eventually, the top-end oil-control problem was solved through the introduction of cup-type valve-spring covers with an oil return line, though no documentation exists to indicate when this solution was discovered and implemented. Nevertheless, it must have been after the build date of the pilot production 61 shown with the company founders, because that machine definitely does not have the valve-spring covers.

After assembly, the first pilot production machines were turned over to the engineering department for road testing. Apparently, problems were experienced with the motors: "Most of these first production 61 OHVs were returned to the motor assembly section for reworking," according to Hatfield. The early production line problems were apparently resolved by the December 16 date of the board meeting because, as Hatfield continued, "Most reworking was by this time sufficiently infrequent and minor to be accomplished on the assembly line."

Unfortunately, we don't know what happened to the "ten or fifteen" pilot production machines. It is possible, as other authors have speculated, that some were sent to favored dealers for independent road testing. If so, these bikes may have been the source of the much-repeated stories of "laps full of oil" after even a short test ride, because the pilot production machines almost certainly did not have the valve-spring covers. We know that these bikes were built in calendar year 1935, so the engine cases *should* have included a "35" prefix in the line-bore number stamp (for example, 35-1234). None of the 1936 61 specialists I have contacted has ever seen cases so marked—which, of course, proves nothing, but hints that the bikes were scrapped after testing, that they have

Front and center on the skull-face instrument panel is a Stewart-Warner speedometer with a 100-mph face, which was used only for 1936 on the Big Twins. For 1937, the speedometer was calibrated up to 120 mph because a well-tuned EL could come very close to outrunning the 100-mph speedometer. The dice gearshift knob was included in the Deluxe Solo Group or was available for $0.60 at the time the bike was ordered.

This close-up of the 1936-only shifter gate shows the shift pattern: 1-neutral-2-3-4, from front to back. For 1936 only, the shifter gate slot is smooth sided, without notched detents to hold the lever in gear position. Rather, the tapered top of the spring-loaded plunger shown through the slot, around the shift lever's shaft, engages scallops along the edge of the slot. With this gate, the shifting motion is straight forward or back—no jockeying to the side to clear notched detents.

all disappeared, or that they were marked with "36" line bore numbers.

With the assembly line procedures debugged, it would seem that H-D was ready to begin full-scale production of the 61 OHV. But did production actually begin at this time? Along with this question, many others come to mind: Did pilot production just gradually ramp up after the December 16, 1935, meeting to become regular demonstrator model production, or was production delayed while further changes were instituted to the 61 design or assembly line procedures? If there was a delay, was it caused by the need to solve the rocker-oiling problem? Was the rocker-oiling problem even solved by the time production began? Documentation that answers these questions conclusively has yet to surface, but a few clues to the production timeline have been found in the H-D archives; we'll consider them later.

Given their lack of experience with production OHV systems—and the truly wretched economy at the time—H-D took a big gamble when they introduced their new OHV Big Twin. The company's fears must have been eased somewhat by the enthusiastic reception their new motorcycle received at the dealers' convention, but only the sales year to come would reveal whether American riders would pay extra for the new engine design—and whether the new engine was ready to meet their expectations.

THE 1936 61 OHV

One of the great mysteries associated with the 1936 Knucklehead is the date actual production began. Some say it began in December 1935; others maintain that it wasn't until March or April of 1936. The principals with firsthand knowledge are all dead, and definitive documentation

MILES OF HAPPINESS

Wisconsin
State Capitol
Madison, Wis.

IN THE SADDLE OF A HARLEY-DAVIDSON

Happiness, you bet! To see the scenic wonders of your own state— visit the capitol city—stroll through the great capitol building. You can even make a "Capitol Tour" of several states on your vacation. No time tables to follow—and so economical, the Harley-Davidson way.

Get the thrill of fast getaway—zooming speed—high-stepping power—eye-filling style—and gliding ride that's yours when you own a 1936 Harley-Davidson.

See the new streamline design and up-to-the-minute motor improvements at your Harley-Davidson dealer's. Ask him for FREE Ride. He'll gladly explain his Easy Pay Plans. And send in the coupon—NOW!

HARLEY-DAVIDSON MOTOR COMPANY
Department P, Milwaukee, Wisconsin

Ride a

HARLEY-DAVIDSON

HARLEY-DAVIDSON MOTOR CO., Dept. P, Milwaukee, Wis.
Interested in motorcycling. Send illustrated literature. Postage stamp is enclosed to cover mailing cost.

Name...

Address...

My age is ( ) 16-19 years, ( ) 20-30 years, ( ) 31 years and up, ( ) under 16 years. Check your age group.

from within the H-D archives has yet to surface. If it is there, I couldn't find it on two separate research visits, so I can't offer an answer—though I have uncovered some interesting facts that shed some light on the timeline.

Remember that admonition in the December 2, 1935, dealer news bulletin that "Under no circumstances should this model be ordered as a demonstrator!"? Only a month later, the factory had obviously taken orders for the demonstrators and was well on its way to filling those orders. The January 27, 1936, dealer news bulletin trumpeted: "61 Overhead Twin Demonstrators Now Being Shipped!" The article beneath the headline went on: "Demonstrator orders for the new 61 Overhead Valve Twin are moving out at a healthy rate and production in the factory is gradually picking up." Of course, "healthy rate" and "picking up" are not very illuminating, but they do indicate that 61s were definitely rolling off the production line by the bulletin's deadline date.

And the bikes shipped on or near that deadline date were obviously not the first machines out the door, because that same news bulletin went on to say, "Reports from dealers who have already received their 61 demonstrators indicate that the new model is proving a real sensation and is exceeding all expectations."

Even more revealing is an actual report from a dealer, Kemper Motorcycle Company in Chicago, Illinois, because it reveals that the factory was by this time (late January) allowing the dealers to sell, or at least take orders for, the new 61s: "Just got in the 61 floor sample this A.M. Everybody likes it. Sold one today and expect two more to trade."

We also know that at least one 61 OHV had been shipped as far west as Portland, Oregon, on or before February 2, 1936, because a rider named "Butch" Quirk used a sidecar-equipped 61 to win the 350-mile endurance run sponsored by the Rose City Motorcycle Club, as reported in the March issue of *The Enthusiast*. Surely this bike was shipped from Milwaukee no later than the last week of January.

The February 10, 1936, bulletin showed that favorable reports had been returned to the factory from as far away as California and Texas. The firm of Graves & Chubbuck in Pasadena wrote: "There never has been

a motorcycle put out that has set the boys to talking so much as the 61. The news of its arrival was broadcast by the boys from the treetops, and five hours after its setup there was 120 miles on the speedometer." From Fort Worth came the report that "this is the first machine that no rider or prospect could find fault with, as they have nothing but praise for it." These bikes must also have left Milwaukee no later than the end of January.

The next issue of the news bulletin lends some credence to the notion that the demonstrators were really just the first production configuration machines, and it implies that regular series production began sometime around mid-February. A headline in the February 24 bulletin announced: "We Are Surging Right Along on the 61!" The article beneath said, "Demonstrator orders for the 61 have all been taken care of and we are now making satisfactory deliveries on dealers' subsequent orders."

Apparently, the factory was not yet mobbed with orders by the deadline for the February 24 issue, so at long last the factory began prodding their dealers to get out and sell the 61, since the much-anticipated new model was at last available. The article continued:

We can't guarantee this state of affairs will continue indefinitely, but right now there is no very long delay in getting out orders. If some of your good customers have been under the impression that they couldn't get their 61's for a long time, better tip them off that if they place their order right away, they can get their machine before long. A little later, when the remarkable qualities of the new model are better appreciated and when the real riding season opens, there may be considerable delay in getting deliveries.

About the time the dealer bulletin exhorted the dealers to push the 61 OHV, the new bike received its first official mention in the national press when it was shown in an ad in the March 1936 issue of *The Motorcyclist*. Even in this first ad, however, the 61 was given no special mention, let alone hype. Earlier, in January, the company had not even shown, let alone mentioned, the 61 in the new model introduction issue of *The Enthusiast*. In fact, H-D would make no official mention of the 61 in their own magazine until June 1936.

So where does this leave us? We still can't say for sure when series production actually began, but it probably started slowly in early January and began ramping up from there until late February, when the factory was able to crank out new bikes at least as fast as the orders came in. By that time, the factory was confident enough about the 61 that they were asking their dealers to sell it, but they were still hesitant to give it their usual sales hype. The first hint of such hype came in the June issue of *The Enthusiast*, which featured a back-cover ad for the 61.

Another big mystery is the exact configuration of the demonstrators. Were they regular production machines? Did they have the valve-spring covers? The glowing reports would seem to indicate that they did—how could a rider not fault a motorcycle that slung as much oil as the 61s without valve enclosures reportedly did?

Then comes the mystery of configuration of the first production models—indeed, the configuration of all the 1936 61s. During the production year, many parts of the 1936 61 were changed in subtle and no-so-subtle ways to improve the function of the machine and to fix problems that became apparent as the bikes were used in competition and on the street. A complete list of all the changes for 1936, with even the most cursory description of the parts and what was changed, could easily fill a book of this size. Since the scope of this book is much broader, covering all the Knuckleheads from 1936 through 1947, the discussion presented here is incomplete, by necessity, and will concentrate on the changes that are obvious—or at least important—in describing later model Knuckleheads.

Models and Prices

Although the new OHV model did not appear in the January issue of *The Enthusiast*, which introduced the rest of the 1936 line, order blanks featuring the model had been quietly sent to dealers. The order blanks listed the OHV Big Twin in three versions: the high-compression 36EL Special Sport Solo, the medium-compression 36E Solo, and the medium-compression 36ES twin with sidecar gearing. All were listed at a retail price of $380, but this was without such essential equipment as a jiffy

stand or a steering damper. These items were available at additional cost or as part of the option groups. Interestingly, a Model 36EM "Twin Motor For Midget Car Racing" is listed in the back of the book, *The Legend Begins*, published by H-D, but I haven't been able to uncover any further details on the motor.

Wheelbase for all models was 59.5 inches and weight was 515 pounds. The main differences between the models was in compression ratio and gearing. The EL engine was fitted with high-compression pistons for a compression ratio of 6.5:1 and a power output of forty horsepower at 3,800 rpm, according to H-D specifications. The E and ES engines were fitted with medium-compression pistons for a compression ratio of 5.66:1 and a power output of thirty-seven horsepower at 3,800 rpm. Interestingly, the compression ratios for the E and ES are listed as being the same, even though the ES was fitted with 0.050-inch compression plates that should have lowered both compression ratio and power. The E and EL were fitted with a twenty-three -tooth engine sprocket, a thirty-seven-tooth clutch sprocket, a twenty-two-tooth transmission sprocket, and a fifty-one-tooth rear sprocket, for an overall ratio of 1:3.73. On the ES with a four-speed transmission, the engine sprocket was changed to twenty teeth, for an overall ratio of 1:4.29. On the ES with the three-speed-with-reverse transmission, the engine sprocket was changed to nineteen teeth, for an overall ratio of 1:4.51.

A four-speed transmission was standard, but a three-speed transmission could be ordered at no additional cost. For $5 extra, the three-speed-with-reverse transmission could be ordered. Early in the year, only standard handlebars were available, but speedster handlebars became available March 3, 1936.

Two option groups for solo machines were offered. The Standard Solo Group included the front safety guard, steering damper, ride control, and jiffy stand; it listed for $14. The Deluxe Solo Group included all the items in the standard group, plus the Chrome Plate Group (chrome handlebars, headlamp, kickstarter lever, muffler—but not the muffler clamps, exhaust pipes, clutch-inspection cover, and safety guard), fender lamp, stoplight, dice shift knob, foot-pedal rubbers, and saddlebags and hangers; it listed for $34.50.

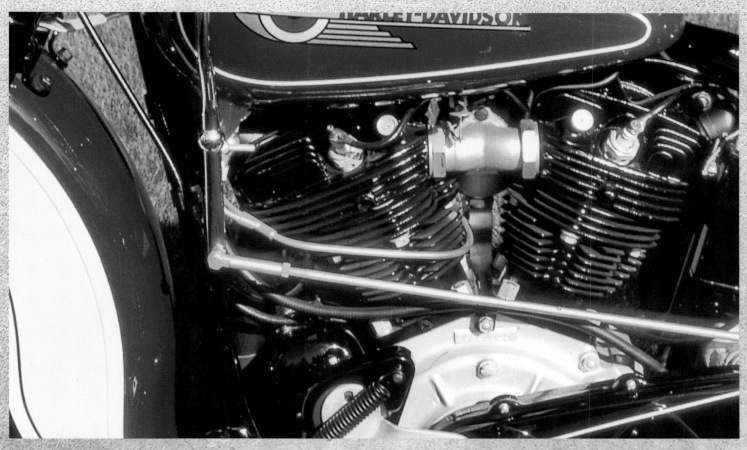

This bike shows the second version of the crankcase. Note the eared boss on each side of the top crankcase stud and the hex-headed plug in the larger-diameter timing hole. Rubber spark plug caps are a functional update for a bike that is ridden frequently, but they're not correct. Note the primer cups just to the inside of the V from each spark plug. A special gas cap was used in conjunction with these caps to prime the intake tract with fuel for cold starting. This bike also retains the cup-type valve-spring covers.

STYLING

Production 1936 61 OHVs carried on the same sleek styling that had been so obviously right on the 1935-serialed 61 shown at the dealers' convention. The new machine featured smooth, streamlined, almost organic lines from front to rear. Perhaps more than any other feature, the styling of the 1936 61 shaped the future of H-D. For model year 1937, all H-D models from the 45 to the 80 were updated to look like the 61.

The basics of this style carried through on all H-D Big Twins through the mid-1960s. It became more and more muted in the 1970s but was revived almost in its entirety on the Heritage Softails beginning in the mid-1980s and helped spark a second renaissance for the company. In the 1990s, the styling cues set on the 1936 61, which proved once again so popular for H-D, were also imitated by the Japanese manufacturers on their increasingly Harley-like and popular big cruisers.

GAS TANKS

The twin, saddle-type gas tanks were the most obvious styling improvement on the new OHV models. Gone were the boxy lines of the earlier H-D Big Twin tanks, replaced by rounded, teardrop-shaped tanks that carried through the tapered line traced by the frame from steering head to rear axle. Each tank has its own separate filler cap and petcock. The left tank holds 2.0 gallons, while the right holds 1.75 gallons. Switched to the down position, the petcocks retain a reserve capacity of ½ gallon in each tank. Switched to the up position,

Classic lines made even the base model an aesthetic marvel. Upgrades, such as the chrome-plated exhaust, were available as part of the Deluxe Solo Group, but the muffler hangers were still painted black when they left the factory. It also has the later, one-piece front safety bar. Early machines like this one were probably fitted at the factory with the three-piece safety bar.

the reserve capacity is available to take the rider those last miles to the next gas station. The left gas tank has a mounting lug for the gearshift-lever pivot and threaded holes for the shifter gate.

INSTRUMENT PANEL

Perched atop the tanks is a stylish, all-new instrument panel that encloses the speedometer, ammeter, oil-pressure indicator, and ignition switch. The shape of the panel suggests the shape of a skull—with the large round opening at the front for the speedometer being the cranium, the two gracefully curved apertures for the ammeter and oil pressure indicator serving as the eye sockets, and the round opening for the ignition switch being the mouth. For this reason, it's been nicknamed

the "skull-face" instrument panel among enthusiasts. The panel was painted black on the outside and white on the inside.

Skull-face-style panels were used on 1936–1938 61s, but the 1936 panel is unique in that it lacks a hole for a speedometer light switch (a small hole just aft of the ignition switch hole) that appears on the 1937 and 1938 panels. If a speedometer with a trip odometer was originally fitted, a hole was drilled in the right side of the panel for the trip odometer reset stem. A rubber grommet was fitted over the stem to keep moisture from getting inside the panel through the reset stem hole.

The 1936 61 was the first H-D Big Twin to be fitted with a speedometer as standard equipment, and the speedometer was given pride of place at the front of the instrument panel. Built by Stewart-Warner, the 100-mph speedometer has a brass face plate with etched silver plating for a background. The numerals 10 through 100 are in black, with long hash marks for the numerals and short hash marks in between for the intermediate 5-mph positions, also in black. A black pointer revolves around a pivot in the center of the face. The odometer window is forward of the pointer pivot. On tripmeter-equipped speedometers, the main odometer window displays five digits, all for miles and none for tenth-miles, in black numerals on a white background. On non-tripmeter speedometers, the odometer displays six digits, five for miles (in black numerals on a white background) and one for tenth miles (in red numerals on a white background). The tripmeter window (if a trip odometer was fitted) is aft of the pivot and displays three digits, two for miles (in black on a white background) and one for tenth miles (in red on a white background). A black H-D bar and shield is aft of the odometer. The glass is flat, and the bezel around the glass is chrome plated. The 100-mph speedometer was a 1936-only part for the 61. In stock form, a well-tuned 61 could just about bury the speedometer needle, so for 1937 the speedometer face was revised to read up to 120 mph.

The ammeter and oil-pressure indicator are situated aft of the speedometer, the ammeter to the left and the oil indicator to the right. The ammeter's needle indicated charge or discharge rates from plus-15 to minus-15 amperes. The oil pressure indicator was little more than a mechanical version of the "idiot lights" that later became common. When the engine was off or oil pressure fell below 4 psi, the word "OFF" became visible through the indicator window. When oil pressure was above 4 psi, the word "RUN" became visible. The indicator was operated by a small oil line that connected the indicator to the oil pump. The ammeter and mechanical oil pressure indicator were used on 1936–1937 61s.

Aft of the indicators is the ignition switch. The ignition switch is key lockable and has four positions (left position routes electricity to the front fender lamp and tail lamp, the center position is off, the next position to the right is for running the bike without lights, and the rightmost position is for normal operation with lights on).

FENDERS

The swoopy, valanced front and rear fenders on the 1936 61 are two of the few examples of parts carried over onto the new model from the Series V side-valve Big Twins. These fenders, first introduced on the 1934 models, look more at home on the sleek new 61 than they do on the Series V machines, which makes one wonder whether they were conceived as part of the overall design effort for the 61. Both fenders are constructed out of the center crown piece and spot-welded side valances.

The front fender is attached to the fork by two braces on each side. Front and rear braces are riveted to a common brace clip on each side, and the brace clip bolts to the fork's rigid legs. Each brace is formed from a single piece of steel about ⅝ inch wide, with the center section riveted to the inside surface of the fender and the left and right legs extending down to the brace clips. The attachment of the brace to the fender is reinforced by a butterfly-shaped plate spot welded over the center of each brace and fender, on the bottom side of the fender. These reinforcements were used for 1936–1938. The rest of the fender was carried over largely unchanged through the end of Knucklehead production (in 1939, stainless-steel fender trim was added, and the braces were made wider in late 1946).

The rear fender is hinged so that the rear section can be swung up and out of the way to change the tires more easily. Like the front fender, the rear fender has two fender braces on each side that are riveted to a brace clip. The front brace is one piece, like those on the front fender, riveted to the underside of the fender and reinforced with a butterfly plate. It attaches to the fender just in front of the fender hinge. The rear brace consists of three pieces that form a detachable brace that can be unbolted to allow the hinged rear fender section to be swung up and out of the way.

The rear mount for the rear chain guard is unique to the 1936 61 (although a similar mount is used on the side-valve twins). The mount is riveted to the rear fender's left front brace. On 1937 and later 61 fenders, the mount was made part of a redesigned left-side brace clip.

This kickstarter cover was introduced in midyear and has a boss for the transmission vent, just visible above the starter spring. The large shaft rising vertically out of the top of the cover connects to the clutch release lever on the outside of the case and to the release fingers on the inside of the case. The chrome-plated kickstarter arm was included in the Deluxe Solo Group or as part of the Special Chrome Plating package offered separately for $13.50. The cadmium-plated "hockey puck" inboard of the kicker arm is the stoplight switch, also included in the Deluxe Solo Group. A chain connected the switch's pull to the brake rod.

PAINT AND GRAPHICS

The paint and graphics on the 1936 61 OHV were nothing short of stunning. The gas tanks were painted a solid color, without panels, but with a contrasting pinstripe that curves gracefully around the art deco transfer on the side of each tank. The fender crowns were painted the same color as the tank, but the fender valances and braces were painted the color of the tank pinstripe. The valance panels wrapped around the front tip of the front fender and around the rear tip of the rear fender. A pinstripe of the main color parallels the curve of the valance's lower edge, about an inch up from the edge. Some bikes shown in the black-and-white photos taken in 1935 and 1936 clearly show a second pinstripe that separates each fender's main section from its panel; others don't. Was the upper pinstripe painted on standard-paint bikes for the whole year or for only part of the year? Or only with certain color combinations? And what color was the upper pinstripe? Dave Minerva, owner of an original-paint 1936 61 in the Venetian Blue and Croydon Creme combination reports that the upper pinstripe on his bike is gold.

Standard 1936 color choices were Sherwood Green with silver panels and wheel rims, Teak Red with black panels and red rims, Dusk Gray with Royal Buff panels and rims, Venetian Blue with Croydon Cream panels and rims, and maroon with Nile Green panels and rims. If one of these fetching color combinations didn't appeal to the buyer, custom colors were also available.

The new EL was a rakish machine from any angle. Shown is the 1936-only slash-cut air-intake horn. This air horn (not a filter) attaches to the carburetor with two screws. Early-1936 carburetors have a two-hole mounting boss for the air horn, but later carburetors have a four-hole boss for the accessory round air cleaner, which attaches with four screws. The carburetor should be nickel plated, and the removable cap at the bottom of the fuel strainer (shown just below the air horn) should have cross-hatched, rather than straight, knurling.

The dealers were well informed that just about any combination of colors and designs was available for the asking. The January 27, 1936, dealer bulletin featured the headline, "Please be explicit about special color specifications!" The accompanying text suggested that dealers describe thoroughly or even send a sketch for any special panels, striping, lettering, or designs the customer desired on his or her new machine.

Photos from the period show a wide variety of paint schemes on new machines, suggesting that many buyers took advantage of the option. Some were all white, with just the pinstripes on the tank and panels. Others had solid-color tanks (without even the pinstriping) or VL-style thick tank stripes (the February 1937 *The*

Motorcyclist shows a photo of "Red" Wolverton's 1936 61 with these stripes). Other riders didn't care for the color-matched wheel rims and chose black-painted rims or even cadmium-plated ones. Surely there is enough documentable variety to give any Antique Motorcycle Club of America (AMCA) judge heartburn.

THE KNUCKLEHEAD ENGINE

The 1936 61 was more than just a styling exercise. It was a completely new motorcycle with features that were modern in almost every way—features that proved so functional that many are still in use on Harley Big Twins today. And most of these were in the motor.

Before we get heavy into the details of describing the individual parts and the myriad details of what changed during 1936, let's discuss the fundamental design of H-D's new motor, little of which did change during that first year—and little of which has changed on H-D Big Twins to this day. The 1936 61 was powered by a forty-five-degree V-twin with a bore of $3^5/_{16}$ inches and a stroke of $3\frac{1}{2}$ inches, for a total displacement of 60.32 ci (988.6cc). H-D's copywriters naturally rounded this displacement up to 61 ci, the origin of its common name during the era. Almost every part in the engine was new, the result of the relentless pursuit of the two main design goals Bill Harley had set for it: OHV cylinder heads and a dry-sump, recirculating oil system. Neither overhead valves nor recirculating oil systems were revolutionary features on motorcycles then, but they represented a big, long-overdue step forward for H-D in 1936. Since these features drove the overall design of the new motor, let's examine them first.

OHV Cylinder Heads

Overhead valves had become common on British and European road bikes such as those built by Ariel, BMW, Brough, Douglas, Matchless, Triumph, and others in the late 1920s and early 1930s. These companies had switched to the new system because overhead valves provide a straighter path into the engine for the fuel-air mixture supplied by the carburetor and a straighter path out of the engine for the spent exhaust gases, resulting in higher volumetric efficiency for greater engine power from a given engine displacement.

Overhead valves had even been tried on American machines before 1936, but mostly on limited-production racing iron built by Cyclone, Indian, and even H-D. Harley had also used overhead valves on some of their small singles, but overhead valves were strangely absent from the big American twins until the debut of the 1936 61 because this greater efficiency came at the price of greater complexity, which meant greater manufacturing expense and the potential for problems. The OHV system H-D chose—two valves per cylinder, operated by a train of rockers, pushrods, and a cam mounted in the crankcase—seems like pretty low-tech stuff by today's standards, but the system was thoroughly modern for 1936.

The 1936 61's cylinder heads are cast iron and are virtual mirror images of each other, with the intake ports of each pointing to the center of the V formed by the cylinders and the exhaust ports pointing out from the V. The intake ports are fitted with a removable intake nipple that threads into the intake port and is locked in place with a rivet. The outer portion of each nipple is also threaded, and the nuts that secure the intake manifold to each head thread onto this portion of the nipple. The exhaust header pipes slip inside a flange in the exhaust port.

The combustion chambers are hemispherical (a configuration later made famous on the high-performance Chrysler Hemi engines of the 1950s and 1960s). Each head carries two overhead valves set at an included valve angle of ninety degrees. Valve seats and guides are replaceable. On the left side of each head is the spark plug hole. Also on the left side of the head, but on the underside of the lowest cooling fin, is the casting number 119-35 (front head) or 119-352 (rear head). On at least some of the 1935-serialed OHV motors—and possibly some of the very early 1936 cylinder heads—the casting numbers were raised from the surface of the fin; on later heads, the numbers were recessed into the fin.

Each head and its attached rocker housing also provide support for the rocker-arm shafts. The right side of each head has three lugs on the right side for mounting the aluminum rocker housing that gives the engine its shape and provides the right-end support for the rocker-arm shafts. On the left side of each head, inboard of the spark plug hole, is a ninety-degree, V-shaped bracket that provides the support for the left end of the rocker-arm shafts. This bracket is integral with the head casting. Each "ear" of the bracket is rounded off on top and has a rocker shaft hole on the centerline near the rounded top.

The rocker shafts insert through the holes in the ears and are fixed in place by a nut. Each ear also has a short reinforcing rib rising vertically (with its axis at a forty-five degree angle to the axis of the bracket) from the base of the V to about the height of the head's cooling fins.

To the rear of the spark plug hole, on the front cylinder head, and to the front of the spark plug

This view shows the mounts for the updated safety guard and the sidecar lugs on the frame. Note the accessory tire pump mounted along the frame's right downtube.

Close-up of the front brake mechanism. It allowed for both solo use and driving with a sidecar.

hole, on the rear head, is a round, cast-in boss. The bosses were drilled and tapped for the optional primer cups, which seem to have been fitted to most low-serial-number 1936 61s but not to many later machines. Turning the primer cup opened a passage to the intake port, into which a shot of raw gas could be squirted from the special priming gun in the right gas tank cap to ease the task of starting the bike on a cold day. Primer cups on the early 61s were a curious holdover from the days of truly primitive carburetors; they seemed archaic and out of place on the sleek, new machine. If the primer cups were not ordered, the holes are plugged by a screw.

Rocker Arms and Shafts

Each valve is opened by its own rocker arm and closed by a set of nested, coil-type valve springs. Each rocker arm rotates on its own shaft. The rocker arm shafts are threaded at each for fixing the shaft to the cylinder head and to the rocker box. Oil for the rocker and valve is carried by the rocker shafts through a ring groove around the shaft's right end, a central passage that ends at an oil passage on the left end of the shaft, and along a groove on the bearing surface of the shaft.

Each rocker arm casting has two arms, a pushrod arm and a valve arm, which are on opposite ends of the casting and point in opposite directions. The valve arm ends in a radiused pad, which is the surface that bears on the top of the valve stem. The pushrod arm's end is fitted with a replaceable pushrod ball socket, which is the surface that bears on the top of the pushrod. The bottom end of the pushrod socket is a ball end that slips into the concave top end of the pushrod. Each rocker is drilled for an oil passage that picks up oil from the bearing surface and carries it to an opening near the valve arm pad to lubricate the valve stem.

Valve-Spring Covers

The key to finally solving the oiling mess that had been the bane of the prototype and preproduction 61s lay in integrating the two systems that defined the new motor: overhead valves and recirculating oiling. This was done through the design of a clever new cover for each valve that catches the oil from the valve gear and returns it to the engine.

Each cover consists of an upper and a lower section. The lower cover is basically a stamped-steel cup with a center hole through which the valve guide is pressed to secure the lower cover to the head. A steel oil return line from each cover connects to the left side of the aluminum rocker housing. The upper part of the cover is a stamped cap with a slot through which the valve arm extends to push on and open the valve, and the cap is secured with a light press-fit over the lower cup. The rocker arms remained largely exposed because the valve-spring covers enclosed only the end of each rocker's valve arm.

After lubricating the rocker arms and valve stems, the oil drips into the lower valve-spring cover. A return line is attached at the low point of the cover, and engine vacuum sucks the accumulated oil out the lower valve-spring covers and back into the engine.

These covers were the 1936 61's most controversial and troublesome feature. When the oil supply to the rocker mechanism was properly adjusted to supply just enough oil to keep the valves from squeaking, relatively little oil escaped the covers. Problems were mostly the result of dirt and water sucked into the covers through the valve arm opening by the same engine vacuum that scavenged the oil out of the lower covers. This dirt and water accumulated inside the covers, mixing with the scavenged oil to form an abrasive sludge that contributed to valve guide wear; it was sucked into the engine, where it remained in circulation until the next oil change. Of more immediate concern, the sludge sometimes clogged the return line so that oil filled the valve-spring cover and spilled over onto rider and machine.

Yes, the design of these covers was less than perfect, but they were certainly better than no covers at all. Remember, the covers were a last-minute fix, added sometime after the preproduction models were built in late 1935 but before the bulk of production bikes were built. Consensus among most 1936 61 aficionados seems to be that most production 61s were fitted with the valve-spring covers. This conclusion is based on the fact that no shop dopes have surfaced with retrofit instructions to add the covers to machines not fitted with them at the factory, and the rave reviews the dealers sent back to the factory about the very first production machines in late January and early February 1936 suggest that these machines had the covers. But others think the very first production machines lacked the covers, and at least one owner reports that he has an early 61 that was never fitted with the covers because none are on the machine and the rocker housings were never drilled for the return oil lines.

It is interesting to note that the break-in instructions for the 61, dated April 14, 1936, instruct riders to "Put a few drops of oil around upper end of valve guides, particularly inlet valve guides." This implies that the valve-spring covers were not yet fitted at the time the instructions were written, because the valve guides are not readily accessible when the covers are fitted, and the rear-exhaust cover is almost impossible to remove when the motor is in the frame.

Which faction is right? Until definitive proof surfaces, I won't weigh in with an opinion on the issue, but I will say this: If the oft-repeated stories about the early 1936 61's propensities for coating the rider's legs with oil are true, they could just as easily be attributed to clogged return lines or maladjusted oiling as they can to a lack of valve-spring covers.

I'll also cite a couple of documents that provide a "no-later-than" date for introduction of the covers.

The first is *Shop Dope No. 140*, dated April 20, 1936, that mentions that "Overoiling will be indicated by oil splashing from the spring covers." The second are the patent drawings for the oiling system submitted on William S. Harley's behalf by the law firm of Wheeler, Wheeler, and Wheeler on May 16, 1936. These drawings show valve-spring covers, but the covers are shaped differently than those on the production machines, and the oil return lines join together. The common line winds around one of the covers so that the viewer cannot see where it connects to the engine, but it appears *not* to attach to the rocker housing (where the return lines from the production covers are attached).

Rocker Housings

Besides being an integral part of the styling for the engine, the aluminum rocker housing attached to each head serves three purposes. First, it supports the rocker shafts. Second, it serves as the conduit that distributes oil to the two rocker assemblies. And third, it routes engine vacuum to the valve spring covers for use in returning the oil to the engine.

To support the right end of the rocker shafts, each rocker housing has two tunnels from the right side to the left side. At each end, the tunnel openings are about 1½ inches. The left side of the rocker tunnels is sealed by a cork seal sandwiched between two steel washers and held in place by a spring clip, which is inserted into a groove around the left side of the rocker tunnel opening. The right end of the shaft tunnel on the early 1936 61s is covered by a round, slightly domed, chrome-plated cover that is fastened to the right end of the rocker shaft by a small center screw. These covers are the "knuckles" of the early rocker housings. On later 1936 61s, the round covers and rope packing were replaced by large, chrome-plated nuts that threaded onto the exposed right end of the rocker shaft and a small seal.

Passages in each rocker housing route the oil to the rocker shafts. Oil return lines from the valve spring covers attach to the left side of the housing, which is drilled through to the pushrod tunnels that rise upward from the bottom of the housing. The return oil also provides the only lubrication to the pushrod ball sockets. The oiling and scavenging systems are discussed in more detail in their own section later in this chapter.

Prototype, preproduction, and possibly very early rocker housings are not drilled for the oil return lines because valve spring covers were not fitted. Early housings were drilled for the fittings, but the castings did not have bosses around the holes. Sometime during the production run, the castings were modified to include the bosses, and an air nipple was added to the front rocker housing. This air nipple is used to blow obstructions out of the return oil lines from the valve spring covers; it will be discussed in more detail later in the chapter.

Pushrods, Pushrod Covers, Tappets, and Tappet Blocks

The tappets, one per pushrod and valve, have a roller lower end that follows the eccentric surface of each camshaft lobe and converts the eccentricity into vertical motion. The tappets rise and fall within the two cast-iron tappet guide blocks (one per cylinder) attached to the top of the right crankcase to transfer the up-and-down motion to the pushrods, which then transfer the motion to the rocker arms.

Each pushrod is fully covered by a two-piece, telescoping pushrod cover with cork seals. The unflanged bottom of each lower cover nestles inside one of the ridged crowns of a tappet guide and rests on a cork seal. The flange at the top of each lower cover is fitted with another cork seal, a washer on top of the seal, a spring on top of the washer, and a spring cap on top of the spring. The lower end of the upper cover fits inside the spring cap and seal.

Each upper cover has a flange at its top end that slips inside a pushrod tunnel in the bottom of the rocker housing and is sealed with a cork washer. The upper and lower covers are prevented from telescoping together by a spring-cap retainer that bears against the flange at the top of the top cover and against the spring cap that rests atop the lower cover. When the retainer is removed, the upper cover can telescope inside the lower cover so that the adjuster screw on the tappet can be accessed during valve lash adjustment.

Completely new from the ground up, the 1936 EL—the Special Sport Solo model—introduced Harley-Davidson's first 61-cubic-inch, overhead-valve V-Twin engine, which the company claimed produced forty horsepower. *David Blattel*

The new OHV system wasn't perfect, and many parts of it changed that first year and in the years that followed. But the valve gear gave the 61 unprecedented performance for an American production twin. Even in its purposely mild state of tune, the OHV engine could propel the 61 to an honest 95 mph. Unfortunately, it didn't remain the fastest American twin for long. That title was wrested from Harley's grasp by the 61 ci, OHV Crocker V-twin that appeared later in 1936. While the high-priced Crocker didn't pose any real sales threat to Harley's 61 OHV (probably fewer than twenty Crockers were produced per year), it trounced the Harleys—and Indians, too—whenever they met.

But the superiority of the limited-production Crocker doesn't in any way diminish the importance of what Bill Harley and his design staff had accomplished. After all, the Crocker firm is long gone, while H-D thrives, and the OHV configuration Harley used into the 1990s has many more similarities to the configuration set on the 1936 61 than it does differences.

PRESSURE OILING AND VACUUM SCAVENGING SYSTEMS

Like overhead valves, recirculating oil systems had been in use for many years before 1936, when the 61 OHV introduced the feature to the Harley lineup. Unlike overhead valves, recirculating oil systems had been common even in America. Harley's main competitor in the US market, Indian, had introduced the feature on their big twin Chief in 1933—and Indian's advertisements and sales brochures often pointed to this feature as evidence of the superiority of their machines, which no doubt fueled the competitive fires in the boardroom in Milwaukee. Although H-D was just playing catch-up with this feature, catch-up was all that was really needed because the OHV top end of the motor put H-D in the technological lead against Indian, and Indian didn't survive long enough to close the gap.

The recirculating oil system Bill Harley and his staff designed for the 61 is of the dry-sump type, meaning that the oil is stored in a separate tank and not in the engine's sump. Dry-sump systems had been used on

many other motorcycles, including Indian, but few of the period were as elegant as Harley's turned out to be. Bill Harley was granted patent 2,111,242 for this oiling system on March 15, 1938.

Oil Tanks

One of the main problems for designers of motorcycle dry-sump systems had always been the location of the oil tank. The tank had to be accessible so the rider could check, add, and change the oil, but it also had to be close to the pump to reduce problems with routing vulnerable oil lines. It also had to be large enough to hold a usable oil supply. Some manufacturers had taken the easy way out and haphazardly hung the oil tank to a frame downtube or anywhere it would fit. These systems worked, but they tended to detract severely from the looks of the machine. Others, including Indian, had partitioned the fuel tank to hold the oil. This, too, performed acceptably, but the oil lines tended to be long and the oil tank's capacity came at the cost of fuel capacity.

The best dry-sump systems were on the British OHV models of the late 1920s and early 1930s, such as the Norton Model 18 and Sunbeam Model 90, which had their oil tanks under the seat, an area that was close to the rear of the engine. Bill Harley chose this location also.

What set Harley's design apart was the way it perfectly blended form and function. The one-gallon oil tank on the 61 is U-shaped, with the open end of the U pointing to the rear. It is perfectly placed to deliver oil by the shortest route to the oil pump, but it also wraps around the battery, hiding its blocky shape from view and contributing to the rounded, streamlined, almost organic lines of the bike. This classic, functional styling cue still contributes to the "Harley look" on such current models as the Heritage Softail.

During its development and first year, the Knucklehead oil tank evolved through at least four versions. The first version, apparently used on some of the prototypes and maybe a few other very early machines, has smooth top and bottom surfaces. It is also identified by one banjo-type fitting at the right rear for the oil feed line to the pump, two banjo-type fittings at the front for the oil

This was an era when riders couldn't just pick up a cell phone and call for repair. This stylish toolbox could carry enough tools for roadside emergencies.

return and vent lines, a filtering screen at the front of the right lobe of the oil tank, and a plugged hole on each side of the tank. The fittings and plugs are welded in place.

The second type of oil tank, used on some early machines, is just like the first, except that it does not have the welded-in plugs on the sides. Later in the year, a third type was introduced. This tank differed from the second in that its top surface was embossed with reinforcements. Still later, the fourth type was introduced. The fourth type has the embossed top of the third type, but the banjo fittings are swaged on, not welded. A decal with oil change instructions was attached to the front right side of the oil tank, below the oil return and vent fittings. These oil tanks and the oil change decal were used only in 1936. At least, some of the 1936 61s were fitted with a dipstick that differs slightly from

dipsticks used in later years. The 1936-only dipstick has a longer ridge, which runs from edge to edge.

Oil Pumps

The all-new, gear-type pump on the 1936 61 is the heart of the recirculating oil system. The pump is contained in a separate housing attached to the outside of the rear end of the gear case and is really two pumps in one—a pressure-feed pump to force oil throughout the engine, and a scavenge pump to return oil to the oil tank. The oil pump body and cover are cast iron and are painted silver.

The oil tank is mounted higher than the oil pump, so gravity assists the pump in drawing oil through a feed line from the back of the oil tank to the oil pump inlet, where the gears of the pump force it to the pressure side of the pump. When oil pressure reaches about 1.5 psi,

There was no better-looking bike in all the world in 1936 than Harley's EL. Some would say that, even though 80 years have passed, its look has never been matched.

the oil unseats the ball in the check valve (which prevents oil from flowing out of the oil tank and into the crankcase while the engine is shut off) and flows to a branched passage. One branch leads to the oil feed passages in the crankcase, and the other to the maximum pressure regulating valve (which remains closed until the oil pressure reaches about 15 psi, when the oil unseats the valve's check ball and bleeds off past the valve to the gear case). The oil pump also directs a small amount of oil to lubricate the primary chain and to actuate the oil pressure indicator on the instrument panel.

Bottom-End Oiling

Oil to the lower end is forced through passages in the pinion gear shaft to lubricate the gear shaft bearings and lower connecting rod bearings. After lubricating these parts, the oil is slung around by the spinning flywheels, forming an air-oil mist that helps lubricate the cylinder walls, wrist pins, and left main bearing.

The flywheels spin clockwise (when viewed from the right side of the powerplant), so flywheel action tends to sling a lot of lubricant on the rear cylinder's walls but little on the front cylinder's walls. To counteract this tendency, H-D engineers used a system of baffles to create more vacuum under the front piston when it rises (which

draws in more of the air-oil mist to lubricate the cylinder) and to partially block the spray of oil to the rear cylinder. The front cylinder baffle plate completely covers the opening to the cylinder, except for a slot for the connecting rod. The rear cylinder's baffle covers only the rear half of the opening, again, except for a connecting rod slot. This basic configuration for cylinder oiling was used through 1939.

Top-End Oiling

Oil to the top end is carried from the gear case by an external, tubular-steel oil line that bends inward toward the cylinders, hiding itself behind the carburetor. The oil line branches to a fitting on each rocker housing, near the intake rocker-shaft cover. In each cylinder head, the oil flows through a passage in the rocker housing and to the rocker arm shafts. A groove running down the shaft distributes oil along its length to lubricate the rocker bearing. The hollow rocker shaft also carries oil to a passage in the rocker's valve arm to lubricate the valve pads and valve guides.

The oil supply to the valves can be adjusted after removing the large, chrome, domed "knuckle" covers—or later chromed "knuckle" nuts—to expose the right ends of the rocker shafts. Oil supply is increased by turning the end of the rocker shaft toward the valve arm side of each rocker (that is, clockwise for the front cylinder exhaust and rear cylinder intake valve shafts, or counterclockwise for the front cylinder intake and rear cylinder exhaust valve shafts), or it can be reduced by turning it toward the pushrod arm. After lubricating the rocker shafts, the oil bleeds out the valve arm end of the rocker arm (and the oil passage to the intake valve guide on some machines).

"Direct Oil Injection" to the Combustion Chambers

Sometime early in the production run, the rocker arm shaft support brackets on the cylinder heads were drilled with an oil passage to the intake valve guides. The special intake guide fitted to these machines has a groove all the way around its outside diameter and is cross-drilled to distribute the oil to the valve stem. This was apparently an attempt to ensure that the valve guides got enough

This 1936 EL, the 374th built, has round tin covers on its rocker shaft ends. Sometime during the production run, these covers were replaced by large chrome-plated hex nuts. Banks's bike also has the "notched" gear-case cover used on early machines. Note the hole in the surface of the gear case, just aft of the brake pedal. Shown in the hole is one of the two rivets used to attach the breather baffle to the inside of the case. The holes for these rivets were sometimes leaded over; after years of engine vibration, though, the lead plugs sometimes pop out, as these have.

The first Knucklehead was a sleek and slim sports machine, as this view shows. In later years, the basic design set in 1936 gained much weight and girth, along with better suspension and lots of accessories—and it would evolve into the classic American touring bike. Very few bikes built by Harley-Davidson in the last 80-odd years have equaled the looks of the first Knuckleheads.

lubrication, even when the overhead oilers were adjusted for the lowest possible oil flow to keep oil spray to a minimum. As you can probably imagine, this was an ill-fated modification, because engine vacuum sucked the oil right into the combustion chambers to foul the plugs and burn into billowing clouds of blue smoke. Ever light on their feet, H-D stopped drilling the passages on new machines after the problem was discovered, sometime during the middle of the production run.

SCAVENGING AND BREATHING SYSTEMS

The heart of the 61 OHV engine breather system is the rotary breather valve in the gear case, which allows crankcase pressure to escape and routes engine vacuum where needed to help scavenge oil. The heart of the scavenge system is the scavenge section of the oil pump, which draws scavenged oil out of the gear case and returns it to the oil tank.

The geared rotary breather valve is driven at crankshaft speed by the cam gear and is timed to open a passage from the crankcase to the gear case each time the pistons are on their down stroke. Crankcase pressure blows accumulated oil and the air-oil mist created by all the rapidly moving parts from the crankcase through the breather-valve opening and into the gear case, where the oil mist lubricates the gears. Early engines were fitted with a breather with a flat screen held to the valve with a stamped metal bracket. Later engines were fitted with an updated valve with a tubular screen that was much more likely to stay in place than was the flat screen.

Crankcase air is vented out of the main gear-case chamber through an integral breather pipe in the gear-case cover and into the breather oil trap chamber at the rear of the gear case. In this chamber, oil is separated from the crankcase air by a screen and by a separator in the breather oil trap. The air is then vented out of the chamber through a separate breather pipe that extends to the left through both crankcases and into the primary chain housing. Air expelled into the primary chain case is still mixed with a minute amount of oil, and this air-oil mixture is deflected onto the chain by the slotted, domed head of the breather pipe.

On the pistons' upstroke, the rotary breather valve is timed to close the passage to the gear case and connect a passage from the crankcase to the pushrod tubes and another passage to the breather oil trap. Vacuum created by the rising pistons pulls oil from the valve-spring covers through the pushrod tubes and into the gear case. Vacuum also sucks out the oil from the breather oil trap into the gear case. Oil trapped in the gear case is sucked out of the case and returned to the oil tank by the oil pump's scavenge section.

Proper sealing of the pushrod covers is vital to keep out dirt and hold in vacuum and return oil. If any of the seals leak, vacuum will be lost, return oil will leak out, and dirt could be drawn in by vacuum. If the seals leak too much, the remaining vacuum will be too weak to pull oil out of the valve-spring covers and back into the engine.

The whole oiling-scavenging-breathing system did its job well, keeping the parts well lubricated, and most of the oil within the engine. A patent application for the system was filed on May 16, 1936, with William S. Harley listed as the inventor. The patent for the system (number 2,111,242) was granted on March 15, 1938. Normal oil consumption on the new 61 varied between two hundred and four hunderd miles per quart, which seems very poor by today's standards, but it was much better than the total-loss oil system of other Harleys.

PISTONS AND PISTON RINGS

The 1936 Knucklehead used conventional cam-ground, slotted, aluminum pistons. They were offered in two versions: high compression and medium compression. The high-compression pistons were fitted to the Model EL and have a high dome, giving a compression ratio of 6.5:1. Medium-compression pistons were fitted to Models E and ES and have a much flatter crown, giving a compression ratio of 5.66:1 (the Models ES are also fitted with compression plates, lowering their compression further, but the specifications do not say by how much). Medium-compression pistons were fitted in 1936 and 1937 only, according to the parts book. Thereafter, the medium-compression Models E and ES were fitted with high-compression pistons with compression plates to lower compression.

The front piston is fitted with two compression rings but no oil control ring, whereas the rear piston is fitted with the two compression rings and an oil control ring. This odd configuration was dictated by the aforementioned clockwise rotation of the flywheels, which slings a lot of oil onto the wall of the rear cylinder, but relatively little onto the wall of the front cylinder. Baffles described earlier in this chapter helped somewhat to even out the oiling to the cylinders.

CARBURETOR AND INTAKE MANIFOLDS

Fuel and air for the 1936 61 OHV motor were mixed by a side-draft-type 1¼-inch Linkert M-5 carburetor with a 1⅙-inch fixed venturi. These carburetors have three mounting holes on their manifold-end flange and two mounting holes in the air horn flange. Sometime during the production run, a four-bolt air horn flange was introduced. The M-5 with two-hole air horn flange was used for 1936 only. The M-5 with the four-hole flange was used from late 1936 through 1939.

On all 1936–1938 Linkert M-5 carburetors, the float bowl lacks a drain plug and has the number "7-64" in raised letters on the inside surface of the bowl. In 1939, a drain hole was added to the float bowl. M-5 carburetors were cast of bronze and were nickel plated, but the bodies were not polished before plating.

The Y-shaped intake-manifold assembly delivers the intake charge from the carburetor to each cylinder head's intake port. The manifold assembly includes the manifold, two large (2 inch) "plumber" nuts to attach the manifold to the each cylinder head's intake nipple, and two brass bushings to seal the plumber-nut connections. Incidentally, the plumber nuts and bushings were among the few parts the designers of the 61 borrowed from Harley's side-valve Big Twins.

The time-proven design outlasted the Knucklehead itself, being used on Harley Big Twins into the 1950s. Some manifolds have a hole drilled in their underside. According to Chris Haynes, these holes were drilled for an aftermarket backfire valve. The valves were apparently of poor quality and eventually leaked, so they were replaced by a bolt to plug the hole. For 1936–1938, the manifold and plumber nuts were unpolished and nickel plated, matching the finish on the carburetor. For 1939, the manifold and nuts were cadmium plated.

The opening and closing of the carburetor's butterfly throttle valve is controlled by the spiral on the right handlebar, acting through a coil-protected control wire.

(For those readers who are more familiar with modern motorcycles, a few terms need to be defined. The twist-grips on vintage Harleys are called "spirals." The two-piece cable that leads from the spiral consists of the "coil" and "control wire." The coil is a protective outer sheath consisting of a coil of wire covered in fabric. The control wire is a cable that slides freely inside the coil.)

H-D motorcycles had long been given a right-hand throttle, while some other motorcycle manufacturers, including Indian, favored left-hand throttles. For those who wanted them—mainly police officers, who wanted to keep their right hand free, say, to shoot their pistols at fleeing suspects—left-hand throttles were optional, usually sold on bikes with right-hand shift levers.

AIR INTAKE HORN AND AIR CLEANER

Rounded at the front, squared off at the sides, and slash-cut at the rear, with three speed-lines embossed along its length, the standard air horn for the 1936 61 was another triumph of art deco styling. It was the mirror image of the air horn used on the 1935 side-valve Big Twins, which is further evidence that the 61 was originally planned as a 1935 model. The air horn was chrome plated and mounted to the carburetor with two screws. Although this horn was beautiful and distinctive, it wasn't really functional because it had no air filter element. Worse, it was prone to rattling itself apart because the two mounting points were insufficient to hold it securely to the carburetor. This air horn was used only for 1936.

For those who wanted or needed an air filter, an optional six-inch round air cleaner with a filter element was available for at least part of the production year. The cover is chrome plated and has the H-D bar-and-shield stamped into the round face and an instruction plate

riveted to the rim. The cover is fastened to the backing plate by four screws, and the backing plate is attached to the carburetor by four bolts. The copper-mesh air cleaner wraps around a mesh support welded to the steel backing plate, which is Parkerized. This air cleaner was also optional for 1937.

CYLINDERS

Cast iron was the standard material for motorcycle cylinders before World War II. It was inexpensive, easily cast into the complex shape of a finned cylinder, and easy to machine for a smooth cylinder bore. The material was also durable, so a liner of another material was not necessary, and its slight porosity allowed it to retain oil for good cylinder lubrication. Consequently, iron was the natural choice for the 1936 61 OHV's cylinders. Nearly fifty years passed before H-D would switch to aluminum cylinders on the Evolution Big Twin, introduced in 1984.

The 61's cylinders were an all-new design. At the top, around the edge of the $3\frac{5}{16}$-inch bore, is a raised ridge that fits into a recess in the head to help seal the head gasket. Outside the ridge is the gasket surface with five head bolt holes spaced around the circumference. A boss for each of the head bolts runs down from the gasket surface through the top four fins. Each head is clamped to the cylinder by bolts inserted from below, through drilled bosses, through holes in the head gasket and into the threaded holes in the head.

The cylinder bases are each held to the crankcases by four studs and nuts, with a base gasket between the cylinder base and the crankcase. External surfaces of the cylinders were painted black. The basic configuration of the 61's cylinders remained unchanged until 1940, when the head bolt bosses were changed so that they passed through the top five fins.

THE BOTTOM END

The 1936 61's lower end was far more conventional for its day than was the top end. Like those on the other H-D Big Twins, the 61's connecting rods run on a common crankpin sandwiched between two flywheel halves, and a pair of mainshafts (one per flywheel half) serves as the axle about which the whole flywheel assembly rotates.

During the production run, an air fitting was added to the front rocker housing that allowed the rider to clear clogged oil return lines from the valve-spring covers by applying air pressure to the nipple. This nipple could also be retrofitted to earlier machines. This bike was never fitted with the nipple.

This view of the Knucklehead's "knuckles" shows the round covers over the right ends of the rocker shafts. A center screw threaded into a hole in the rocker shaft's end and fixed the cover in place. Rope packing behind the cover sealed the end of the shaft. With the covers removed, the rocker shafts could be turned to increase or decrease oil supply to the rockers and intake valve guides.

Each flywheel half is 8⅛ inches in diameter and has a tapered center hole for a center shaft and an off-center tapered hole for the crankpin. These flywheels were used on the 61s from 1936 through 1940.

The front cylinder rod's big end is "forked," and the rear cylinder rod's big end was designed to nestle inside the fork. Forked connecting rods were used on most V-twins of the era. Engine designers liked them because they are narrower than two connecting rods placed side by side, which then allows the engine designer to use a short, stiff crankpin. The only real disadvantage to the knife-and-fork arrangement is that it also puts both cylinders on the same centerline, to the detriment of rear-cylinder cooling. (If the big ends are placed side by side, the crankpin must be longer, but the front and rear cylinders could be offset, allowing a more direct flow of cooling air to the rear cylinder.) The tapered crankpin fits through the big-end bearings of the connecting rods, into the tapered, offset holes on the flywheel halves, and is secured on the outer side of each half by a crankpin nut and lock plate. This basic arrangement was used through 1939.

The mainshaft from the left flywheel is called the "sprocket shaft." It is secured to the left flywheel on the inner side by the sprocket shaft nut and lock plate. Supported by roller bearings in the left crankcase half, the sprocket shaft extends into the primary-chain case to drive the primary-chain sprocket. The sprocket then transfers engine power through a three-row primary chain to the clutch sprocket.

The center shaft from the right flywheel is called the "gear shaft." This shaft consists of two pieces, a stub shaft and a pinion shaft. The stub shaft is secured to the right flywheel on the inner side by the gear shaft nut and lock plate and extends through the roller bearings in the right crankcase. The pinion shaft, attached to the stub shaft by means of an eccentric tongue-and-groove joint, extends into the gear case on the right side of the engine to drive the oil pump, cam gear, breather valve, ignition circuit breaker, and generator. Attached directly to the gear shaft are two gears: the oil pump drive gear and the pinion gear.

The oil pump drive gear is the innermost of the two gears and is machined into the shaft. It is a worm-type

that meshes with a gear on the end of the oil pump drive shaft, to change the direction of drive ninety degrees toward the rear of the bike to turn the shaft for the oil pump. The shaft extends through the rear of the gear case to drive the two-section pump, which is mounted at the rear of the crankcase on the right side.

The outer gear is the pinion gear, which is a separate piece that is press-fit onto the pinion shaft. This small diameter gear is comparatively wide. The width of the pinion gear allows it to mesh with two larger diameter gears that are thin and overlap each other—the cam gear (vertically above the pinion gear) and the intermediate gear (to the right of the pinion gear as viewed from the right side of the bike).

The cam gear turns the single, four-lobed camshaft and drives the rotary crankcase breather valve gear that is aft of the cam gear. The intermediate gear is driven off the inner portion of the pinion gear at half speed. Mounted on the intermediate gear's shaft, on the crankcase side, is another gear that drives (also at half speed) the ignition circuit breaker. (See the discussion of ignition for more details.)

To the right of the intermediate gear is the idler gear. The idler gear transfers drive from the intermediate gear to the generator drive gear. The generator is mounted transversely on the front of the engine, its drive shaft extending into the gear case on the right side of the motorcycle and its end cover on the left. (See the charging system discussion for more details.)

"LIGHTNING" CAMSHAFTS

The 1936 61 came with a new camshaft arrangement that was unlike the arrangement used on the side-valve Big Twins. The side valves had a separate camshaft and timing gear for each valve because the flat valve angle and short pushrods of the side-valve engine prevented the use of angled-in pushrods necessary for a common camshaft. The long pushrods and ninety-degree valve angle of the new OHV engine allowed all four pushrods to be angled in to a single four-lobed cam.

Besides the obvious benefits of reduced manufacturing cost and complexity, the single-cam arrangement ran quieter and gave more consistent and precise timing because only one gear was needed instead of four.

The cams fitted to the 1936 61 OHV are different from most that followed and have gained a reputation for being especially "hot." In later years, these cams were much sought after by savvy performance tuners who knew the cam's reputation and how to pick them out of the milk crates full of lesser cams at swap meets. These special cams are identified by the measures taken to lighten the cam gear—six holes and metal machined away on the front and back. References to these lightening measures and the performance offered by the cam resulted in the description "lightening" being misconstrued into a nickname for the cam: "Lightning."

Some sources report that at least three versions of this cam were offered in 1936. The cam fitted to the early 61s was reportedly so far advanced that the bikes were prone to backfiring as they were kick-started. Sports-oriented riders could overlook the occasional backfire because these cams gave great performance, especially at higher rpm. Later, the cam timing was reportedly retarded to reduce the tendency to backfire. Still later, some say, a third cam was released that had two sets of timing mark, one for solo machines and another for those equipped with a sidecar.

CRANKCASES

All unaltered 1936 61 OHV left-engine cases have a cast-in baffle covering the rear half of the rear cylinder hole (except for the slot running fore and aft for the connecting rod), a full baffle covering the front cylinder hole (except for the con-rod slot), and the casting number 112-35 (in raised numbers) below the primary cover boss. Early 1936 left cases have a small-diameter timing hole, which is usually plugged by a cad-plated, straight-slot screw. Later cases have a larger timing hole (plugged by a cad-plated bolt) and two small raised "ears" above the serial-number boss, one on each side of the hole for the top crankcase stud. This second style of left case remained in use through mid-1939.

Only one style of right crankcase was used in 1936. It has the baffles and the casting number 112-352 below the gear cover. This case was used through 1939.

"LINE-BORING" NUMBERS

At the start of engine assembly, each Knucklehead crankcase set was bolted together and the mainshaft holes were line-bored through both cases at once, ensuring that the holes were in good alignment. The matched set of cases were then each stamped with a "line-bore" number. The number consisted of two digits for the year and four digits to denote the engine's place in the production run, separated by a hyphen. For example, 36-1234 indicated that it was the 234th set of 61 cases line-bored in 1936. In later years, when production was higher, five digits denoted the engine's place in the production run. The line-bore numbers seldom match the serial number because the line-bore numbers were applied at the start of assembly, whereas the serial numbers were applied near the end of final engine assembly. However, line-bore numbers and serial numbers seldom differ by more than 100 or so. The two-digit number apparently indicates the year the case was line-bored, which is not necessarily the model year of the motorcycle. For example, some 1937-serialed cases have line-bore numbers that begin with "36," because they were line-bored in 1936.

GEAR CASE COVERS

At least three different gear case covers are known to have been used on 1936 61s. The earliest style is called a "notched" cover, in reference to the recessed notch at the rear end of the cover. Inside, a steel baffle is riveted onto this cover to shield the inlet to the gear case breather pipe cast into the cover. The rivets securing the baffle were often leaded over at the factory, but the lead plugs work lose from the vibration and heating-and-cooling cycles of decades of use, so the rivets are often visible on the outside of the cover.

Later covers are "smooth," in that they lack the notch of the earlier covers. The first smooth covers still had the riveted-on baffle, with the rivets sometimes showing on the outside of the cover. Still later, the gear-cover casting was revised to feature a cast-in baffle. Rivets were not used on the last style of cover, and it was used on subsequent 61s through 1939.

CHARGING SYSTEM

The 1936 Knucklehead's charging system was one the few systems on the new machine that was carried over from Harley's earlier twins. The system consists of a generator, external generator cutout relay, and a battery.

The generator is the Model 32E six-volt DC unit with a rotating armature, two magnetic field coils (regulating and shunt) fixed to the generator case, and three brushes (positive, negative, and current-regulating) in contact with the commutator. This generator is used without an external voltage regulator because the third brush regulates the current output. Moving the third brush toward the negative brush increases current output, while moving it away decreases output.

Like the plumber nuts discussed earlier, the Model 32E worked so well that it was borrowed from earlier Harleys and passed on to later Harleys, after the Knucklehead engine was discontinued. It was the standard generator for H-D Big Twins from 1932–1952.

For riders who needed more current than the Model 32E could supply—mainly police users with bike-mounted radios—H-D offered an optional generator, the Model 32E2, that had longer armatures and fields to supply the extra current. The Model 32E2 generator is also a six-volt, three-brush design that is used with a cutout relay but without a voltage regulator. It was optional for 1936–1938.

The external cutout relay functions to disconnect the generator from the rest of the electrical circuit until the voltage produced by the generator exceeds battery voltage (preventing the battery from discharging through the generator windings). This cutout relay looks much like a voltage regulator and mounts just forward of the ignition circuit breaker, on the forward part of the right side of the motor. The cutout relay was also carried over from earlier H-D motorcycles (having been in service since 1932). This relay has two terminal posts and is correct for 1936 and 1937 Knuckleheads.

IGNITION SYSTEM

Magneto ignitions were common in the motorcycle industry in 1936, especially on serious sporting machines. Magnetos are simple, light, and relatively trouble free. But

H-D had abandoned the magneto on their Big Twins in favor of a point-and-ignition-coil system with a distributor; the company reasoned that coil-stoked ignitions give a hotter spark at start-up, and they also make the kick-start ritual more of a sure thing, especially in cold weather.

In 1927, they had modified the ignition to create a curious style of coil ignition. Using a clever concept known as "wasted spark," Harley created a coil ignition system that is nearly as simple as a magneto system; it requires just one set of breaker points and one coil to operate both cylinders (no distributor or second set of points and coil). The coil fires both spark plugs each time the points open, igniting the fuel-oil mixture in one cylinder and "wasting" the other spark on the burned gases being expelled from the other cylinder on its exhaust stroke. Naturally enough, H-D chose to fit their new 61 with their wasted-spark system.

Looking much like an automotive distributor, the 61's ignition circuit breaker or timer is mounted to the right of the front cylinder. The timer's main functions are to open the breaker points and time the break so that it occurs at precisely the right instant. Inside the breaker cover is a set of breaker points, a two-lobed cam, and the condenser. The cam lobe for the front cylinder is narrower than the lobe for the rear cylinder. The timer shaft and cam are spun at half crankshaft speed, so the plugs fire at every other stroke.

The ignition timer assembly fitted to the first 1936 61s was basically just a longer version of the timer fitted to the side-valve Big Twins. After motor number 1422 was built, a new timer was introduced. This new timer has larger-diameter ($^{45}/_{64}$ inch, versus $^{5}/_{8}$ inch) holes for the shaft. On both of these timer assemblies, the circuit breaker wire feeds into the side of the assembly through a notch in the side of the timer base, and the wire connects to the top of a terminal on the base. Timers with the notched timer base were used only for 1936; the following year, the timer was revised to route the timer wire out through a hole in the timer housing, which made the wire less vulnerable to chafing.

Mounted on the motorcycle's left side (in front of the oil tank), a single twin-lead ignition coil generates the spark. One spark plug lead goes to the front spark plug and one to the rear plug, but both fire each time the points are opened by the points cam. In greatly updated form—with electronic black boxes replacing the points and advance mechanism—the wasted-spark system is still in use on the 1990s Harleys.

Transmission and Shifter

Just as the OHV motor signaled the dawn of a new age for H-D, so too, did the new bike's transmission—an advanced, four-speed, constant-mesh design that was quieter, stronger, and more durable than the sliding-gear transmissions found on the competing Indian and foreign motorcycles. Although a constant-mesh transmission had been used on a few earlier 45-ci Harleys, the 1936 61 was the first H-D Big Twin to use a constant-mesh transmission.

The all-new transmission was carried in its own housing separate from the engine, and this basic transmission proved to be one of the 1936 Knucklehead's most enduring features. In fact, it was passed on largely unchanged to all the H-D Big Twins through 1964, except for those built during the 1939 model year, when a curious new four-speed offered a hybrid of the constant-mesh and the older sliding-gear types. Optional transmissions included a three-speed and a three-speed with reverse.

TRANSMISSION CASES

The components of the new transmission were housed in at least two different transmission cases for 1936, neither of which had a cast-in support for the kickstarter side of the transmission. The early 1936 case has four frame-mounting studs and is not drilled for the mounting holes for the countershaft end cap fitted to later cases. In mid-1936, H-D began drilling the transmission case for the four countershaft-end-cap screws. The case was supported on the starter side by a bracket attached to the two lower studs for the starter cover and a bolt that butts against the lower frame tube. A new starter-side support bracket was introduced in late 1936. More details on these mounts are provided later in this chapter.

Clutch

The transmission is connected to engine power via a conventional multi-plate clutch and a primary chain.

The Venetian Blue and Croydon Cream paint scheme shown was probably the most popular of its day, and it still is today, judging by the high percentage of machines that are restored to these colors.

Both forks and horn were new designs for 1936, contributing to the bikes' classic lines. The only damping on these spring forks was provided by the optional "ride control" plates, shown here on Banks's bike. Ride control was just friction damping that could be adjusted by tightening or loosening the lower knob. Note the grease fitting pointing forward on the spring perch, above and to the side of the upper horn mount; a fitting is present on each side. Located here from 1936 through 1938, the grease fittings were moved in 1939 to the side of the spring perch and made to point to the sides.

This clutch and drum proved to be nearly bullet-proof, able to handle much more than stock horsepower. Aside from a few changes to the discs, the assembly was carried forward onto the subsequent 61s through 1940.

The clutch disc pack consisted of five fiber friction discs, three flat steel discs, and one "humped" steel disc. The fiber discs have notches on their outer circumference that mate with the splines on the inside of the clutch drum. The flat steel discs have splines on their inner circumference that mate with the splines on the outside diameter of the clutch-driving disc. Drive is transferred through splines on the inside of the clutch drum to the friction discs.

When the clutch is engaged, ten clutch springs force the friction discs into contact with the steel discs, and the steel discs transfer the power to the clutch-driving plate through their splined mating surface on the driving disc's hub's outside circumference. And the driving plate transfers the power to the hub through another splined mating surface, this one on the driving disc's hub's inside circumference.

The disc pack worked well under normal use, but under hard use or lots of stop-and-go driving, the discs sometimes stuck and dragged. Even so, they were carried over onto the early 1937 61s.

In traditional American practice, the clutch was foot operated by a pedal on the left side of the motorcycle. The pedal had toe and heel pads, the operation of which was the opposite of that used on cars and some other motorcycles, including the Indian. Push down on the toe pedal, and the linkage would engage the clutch. Push down on the heel pad, and the linkage would disengage the clutch. The pedal was cadmium plated through about mid-1937, Parkerized thereafter. The foot-operated clutch-release mechanism was used on all Harley Big Twins through 1951.

The pedal connects to the transmission's clutch-release lever by a rod threaded on the front for the clevis; it is slightly flattened at the rear to slip into one of the two slots on the clutch-release lever's end. The release lever is made of two pieces that are brazed together. The larger piece is a round rod with a dogleg bend, and the rod is flattened at the dogleg. The second piece is the right end, which has a square hole that mates with the release-lever stud; this extends through the kickstarter cover to attach to the release finger. This cadmium-plated lever was used for 1936 and 1937.

The weak link in the 1936 61's clutch system was its throwout bearing. Two different throwout bearings were used in 1936 alone, and neither of these proved satisfactory. On the first 1936 61s, H-D reused the six-ball throwout bearing first used on the side-valve 45s, which were introduced in late 1928. While the bearing

The constant-mesh four-speed transmission was all-new for 1936 and would provide the basis for all Harley-Davidson Big Twin four-speeds to follow—except for the 1939 hybrid transmission with sliding second gear.

was adequate for the loads imposed by the 45, it proved to be too weak to stand up to those of the 61, so it was replaced in midyear by a larger bearing with eight balls. This new bearing was used until mid-1938, when it was replaced with a still-larger bearing. And even this bearing wasn't stout enough—it, too, was replaced, for the 1939 model year.

Kickstarter Assembly

The 1936 61 was fitted with a conventional kickstarter assembly that includes a crank arm with pedal and return spring, a starter clutch, and gears to turn the transmission mainshaft and transfer the kickstarting force through the clutch to turn over the engine. The starter clutch disconnects the gears when the crank arm is in its rest position and again at the bottom of the

stroke. If the rider pauses and holds the kicker arm at the bottom of the stroke, there is no danger of the engine kicking back through the crank.

The assembly is housed in the kickstarter cover on the right side of the transmission. At least two covers were used during 1936 production, and the only significant difference between them is that the early 1936 cover has a milled flat (but no boss) for the transmission vent tube, which is located above the starter-crank tunnel, while the late 1936 cover does have a cast-in boss for the vent. The later cover was also used on early 1937 61s.

On both covers, the starter crank tunnel carries a one-piece bushing for the starter crank's shaft, while the outer end of the tunnel is sealed by a cork washer held in a machined-in recess in the boss around the starter

The two best-looking stock paint schemes on any of the Knuckleheads—1936 and 1939. The 1936 is owned by Dave Banks, and the 1939 by Ron Lacey. Note the chrome-plated clutch-inspection cover on Banks's bike. The cover was part of the Chrome Plate Group, which was also part of the Deluxe Solo Group, as was the front fender lamp shown. Note the mount on the front stay for the rear fender. It is the type used beginning in 1937. The correct mount is a separate tab riveted to the back of the stay, about halfway up.

crank tunnel. The tunnel boss is reinforced inside the cover by five ribs around the boss.

Early starters on four-speed transmissions used a twenty-six-tooth starter-crank gear that meshed with a fourteen-tooth mainshaft starter gear. The gears were changed sometime early in the production run to twenty-four teeth on the starter-crank gear and eighteen teeth on the mainshaft gear. This revised gearing was used on all four-speed transmissions through 1947 and on 1939-and-later three-speed and three-speed-with-reverse transmissions.

The starters for 1936–1938 three-speed and three-speed with reverse transmissions use yet another gearing combination: twenty-two teeth on the crank gear and eighteen teeth on the mainshaft gear.

Primary-Chain Housing

A two-piece guard covers the primary chain, keeping dirt off the chain and lubricant inside it. At least two different inner covers and three different outer covers were fitted at various times during the 1936 production cycle.

The inner cover used through mid-1936 lacks an oil drain hole because it is used in conjunction with an outer cover having a drain hole. Later 1936 inner covers are like the previous cover, except that a nipple for a drain-pipe is added to the lower rear surface of the cover and two more reinforcement ribs are stamped in—a medium-length rib aft of the crankcase-breather-pipe hole and an even shorter one just aft that. All inner primary covers were painted black. Drainpipes were cadmium plated.

The first type of outer primary cover was probably fitted to only the preproduction 61s. It is unique in that it has a screw hole on each side of the primary-chain inspection-cover hole. The purpose of these holes is not known, but they probably fastened some sort of baffle. This outer cover also had a drain hole under the clutch derby.

The second type of primary cover used on the 61 is like the previous cover, except that it lacks the two screws that fore and aft of the primary-chain inspection cover. This outer cover was first fitted sometime early in the production run, and may even have been fitted to the first production machines. It, too, has the drain hole. Sometime during the production run, a third outer cover was introduced. The third 1936 outer cover was the same as the second type, except that the drain hole was omitted because this outer cover was used in combination with a new type of inner cover that had a fitting for a drainpipe. This third outer cover was then fitted to all subsequent Knuckleheads through 1940.

Outer primary covers were painted black. Standard chain inspection covers were chrome-plated for 1936 and 1937, but were painted black for the following years (although plated covers were optional for most years). Standard clutch-inspection covers were also painted black, but chrome-plated covers were part of the Chrome Finish Group for 1936 and 1937. Inner and outer covers are fastened together using 10 Parkerized fillister-head straight-slot screws.

FRAME

Harley-Davidson's 1936 Knucklehead came with a frame as different and as modern as its engine. Previous Harley frames had all been single-downtube types that were really just descendants of turn-of-the-century bicycle frames. Single-downtube frames were light and easy to build, but they lacked the rigidity to handle higher weights and more horsepower. The new Knucklehead frame had twin downtubes that cradled the engine in a cage of chrome-moly tubing that stretched from the steering-head forging at the front to the axle-mount forgings at the rear. And its twenty-eight-degree steering-head angle gave a perfect balance of steering and stability with the stock 18-inch wheels and 4.00x18-inch tires.

Unfortunately, the only rear suspension provided was the spring-mounted seat.

The top of each of the two main downtubes was single-butted to a slash-cut, larger diameter tube extending down from the steering head. From the butted joint, each tube sweeps down and back, around the engine and transmission, to join with the axle-mount forging for its side. The backbone tube is larger in diameter than the downtubes and angles down and back from the steering head to join with the seat-post tube. Sidecar mounting loops are brazed to the front side of each downtube, and a mounting strap for the toolbox is brazed between the upper and lower tubes just forward of the right axle clip.

The engine mounts to the frame at three points: to a lug from the backbone tube, to a casting that bridges the down tubes underneath the front of the engine, and at the shelf-like rear motor mount attached to the front side of the seat-post tube. The transmission mounts to a plate that allows the transmission to be adjusted fore and aft to tighten or loosen the primary chain.

Sidecar Mounting Lugs

All production and pilot production 1936 61 frames are thought to have come from the factory with sidecar mounting loops fastened to the front downtubes, but some of the prototype and preproduction frames apparently did not have them, as shown in the disassembly photo of 35E1003. The sidecar lugs also served as the lower mounting point for the three-piece safety guards that were optional for most of the 1936 production year. Sidecar loops on early frames are brazed on, while those on some of the later frames appear to be welded on. When asked how the lugs on one of his frames was attached, Chris Haynes said they appeared to be tack-welded in place and brazed. It is possible that some very late 1936 61s were fitted with the updated frame for 1937 with the new-style sidecar-mount forgings that were introduced for that year. See Chapter 2 for more details on this frame.

"Fifth" Transmission Mount

Anyone who has ever kicked over one of H-D's Big Twins knows firsthand how much force is transferred through the kickstarter's crank arm to the transmission, especially at the end of the stroke, when the rider's full weight bears down on a lever that is hard against its stop. The transmission on all 1936 61s had four studs for fastening it to the frame. Unfortunately, on the kickstarter end of the transmission, the tranny case was not bolted to the frame. Rather, it was loosely supported by what seems to be another one of the underthought quick fixes that were necessary to get the bike into production for 1936: a sheet-metal bracket was bolted to the kickstart cover and an adjustable support bolt extended down from the bracket to butt against the frame tube.

When properly adjusted, the bolt and bracket provide adequate auxiliary support to the four solid mounts on the transmission. But when improperly adjusted, a number of problems can result. If the bolt is not adjusted far enough down to contact the frame, kickstarting loads are transferred to the other transmission mounting studs and to the frame's transmission mounts, eventually tearing the studs loose from the transmission case and forming cracks near the mounts. If the bolt is adjusted too far out, it "cocks" the transmission so that the engine and clutch sprockets are no longer in line, causing binding and accelerated wear.

Harley-Davidson made the kickstarter-end support "idiot proof" late in the 1936 production run by introducing a "fifth," nonadjustable transmission mount to support that end of the transmission. The new mount consisted of a support pad brazed onto the frame and a revised support bracket that was more rectangular in shape and stouter, but which still attached to the lower studs on the kickstarter cover. The bottom of the bracket butted up against the top of the support pad on the frame and a cap screw clamped the two together, providing a fairly good fifth transmission mount.

The new mounting pad and bracket were carried over into 1937 production, but the bracket was eventually replaced by a cast-in lug on the revised transmission case that was introduced in mid-1937. Some authorities say that very late 1936 61s were fitted with the revised transmission case and thus do not use the bracket. This is unlikely, however, because the 1937 parts book states that the second type of bracket, part number 2263-36A,

was used on the later 1936 61 and "first 1937—61", 74", and 80" twins."

Frame Cracking

In keeping with the sporting nature of the machine, the 1936 61's frame was made as light as possible. At 7/8-inch in diameter, the main tubes turned out to be too light. Because of this, the frames were prone to cracking at the seat post, the transmission mount, and on the left rear stay when the machines were ridden hard—especially off-road, as riders of the day often did. Cracks were fixed by welding the broken pieces, either at a dealership or at the factory. If the work was done at the factory, a number was often stamped in the reinforcement webbing behind the seat post.

When a sidecar was fitted, the front downtubes often cracked from the extra torsional strain transferred to the tubes through the sidecar mounting lugs. Anecdotal evidence exists that a fix for the latter problem was sometimes performed at the factory by brazing in a longer slash-cut reinforcement on the downtubes. The reinforcement on these frames extends far below the normal slash-cut joint, sometimes to a point just above the sidecar mounts. At least one example exists of a frame that was apparently fitted with the longer reinforcements at the time the frame was built, as this frame shows no sign of modification. Were these frames built for the ES models for sidecar use? Or for the later ESs? Future research may supply the answer.

The real fix for the problems with frame cracking came in 1937, when a new frame was introduced that was heavier duty all around. Some authorities hold that the new frame was fitted to the very last 1936 61s, citing the fact that many 1936 61 engines reside in these frames today (including the 1936 61 in the H-D collection). Since no documentation exists to prove conclusively when the new frame was first fitted, the most I can offer is an opinion: Some very late 1936 61s may have come with the 1937 frame, but it is more likely that the 1936 engines in these frames are there because the original cracked frame was replaced under warranty with the updated frame. Another possibility is that the owner upgraded the bike at a later date when

Carman Brown's restored 1936 61. Note the holes in the chrome-plate atop the handlebar's center section. These appear only for 1936, and they are one of the many mysteries of the 1936 61. I have never heard a plausible answer for why the holes were drilled.

it cracked or was damaged in an accident. It is unlikely that H-D stocked the trouble-prone 1936 frame as a replacement part.

Toolboxes

The 1936 61 was fitted with a toolbox that is similar but not identical to the one fitted to the side-valve models. It mounts to a bracket on the right side of the motorcycle. The box is rectangular and mounts so that the long dimension is vertical, with a cover held closed by a keyed lock. Box and cover are painted black, and a H-D patent decal is attached to the cover. This rectangular toolbox is correct for 1936–1939 61s.

Forks and Handlebars

The new forks on the 1936 Knucklehead were leading link, spring-suspended forks with about two inches of travel. They differed little in concept from the forks on

previous Harley Big Twins, but they were a bit stouter. Externally, the main difference is that the legs of the rigid fork on the new 61 look smoother and more streamlined because they were made of extruded, oval-section tubing, rather than of the drop-forged I-beams used for the forks on the side-valve Big Twins.

The 1936 61's forks had no built-in damping, but optional friction plates, called "ride control," could be ordered. These plates, one on each side of the fork, could be tightened or loosened for more or less friction, much like the steering dampers of the day. On the 1936–1937 61's ride control, the adjusting knob was on the right side. On later machines, the adjusting knob was on the left side.

Only minor changes were made to these forks from 1936 to mid-1946, when they were replaced by the new "offset" springer forks. Distinguishing features of the early forks include two forward-facing grease fittings on

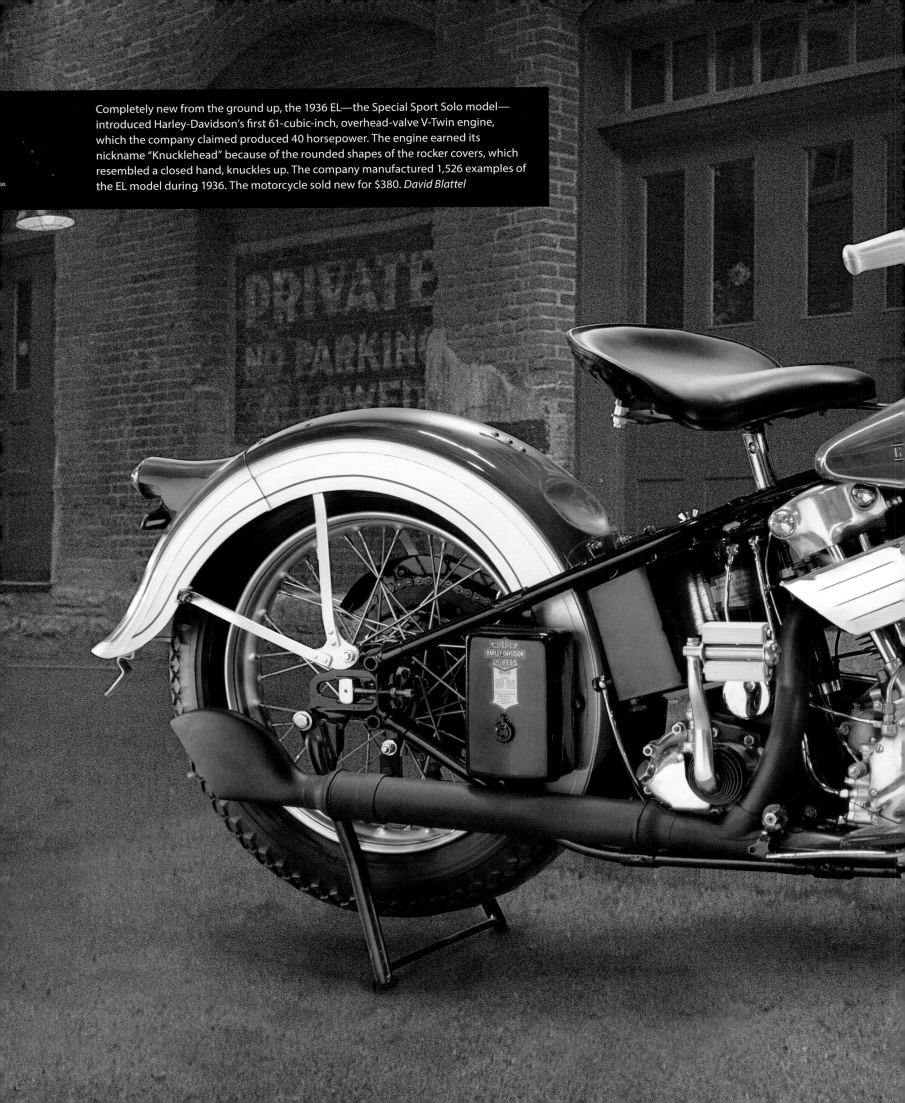

Completely new from the ground up, the 1936 EL—the Special Sport Solo model—introduced Harley-Davidson's first 61-cubic-inch, overhead-valve V-Twin engine, which the company claimed produced 40 horsepower. The engine earned its nickname "Knucklehead" because of the rounded shapes of the rocker covers, which resembled a closed hand, knuckles up. The company manufactured 1,526 examples of the EL model during 1936. The motorcycle sold new for $380. *David Blattel*

In then-current style, the front wheel moved up and down independently of the fender.

the font of the spring-perch forging, and narrow, unreinforced mounting tabs for the front fender. The grease fittings remained in this location until they were moved to the outside left and right edges of the spring perch in 1939 so that the fittings point out to the sides. The narrow fender tabs were used through 1937, but for 1937 they were reinforced by plates spot welded underneath each.

HANDLEBARS AND HAND CONTROLS

The 1936 61's handlebars were also new, to fit the new fork. The left and right bars are brazed to a center forging that has a center hole and two smaller-diameter flanking holes, into which the tops of the fork's rigid-leg tubes slip. Pinch bolts clamp the forging around the fork tubes. At the start of the model year, only the Standard bars were available, but the March 3, 1936, dealer news bulletin announced the availability of new speedster bars for the sport-oriented 61 rider. According to the bulletin, "The rider using them leans forward just a little and presents a race-like, speeding appearance." Speedster bars were available in place of the standard bars for no extra cost after this date. Bars were painted black unless the Deluxe Solo Group or special chrome package was ordered, in which case they were chrome plated.

The inner diameter of each bar end is threaded for a screw that retains the spiral, throttle spiral on the right and spark-control spiral on the right. The outer portion of the spirals shows a $2\frac{3}{8}$-inch-wide chrome band inboard of the plastic grip. Correct grips swell in the midsection and have a pattern of ridges running the length of the grip. Standard grips were white rubber, with optional black grips. Throttle and spark-control coils and control wires are routed through the bars and emerge from holes in the bosses near the ends of the handlebar's center forging. These spirals and grips are correct for 1936–1942.

The left bar also has a headlight dimmer switch, a horn switch, and a front-brake hand lever and bracket. The brake hand-lever assembly consists of an S-shaped, chrome-plated steel lever and a Parkerized lever bracket and clamp bracket. This hand lever and bracket were used from 1936 through 1940.

Continuing Problems

The 1936 Knucklehead was a basically sound design, but a number of circumstances—H-D's understandable eagerness to recoup the new bike's high development costs, the cumulative financial squeeze of the Depression, labor laws that prevented H-D engineers from working overtime—combined to force H-D's management into ordering the new model shipped to dealers in a form that was essentially an advanced prototype. Predictable difficulties ensued, but the company rushed to correct these teething problems with updated parts and tuning information, sometimes modifying a single part three or more times during the production run. The daunting number of such changes made during the 1936 model year attests to the fact that its configuration had been far from finalized when the first bikes were shipped.

The most chronic problem was the same one that is thought to have delayed the 61's introduction for so long—oil control. Even after the valve-spring covers were put into production, oil leaks were still common. One of the main causes of leaks was improper adjustment of the oil supply to each rocker arm. A little well-intentioned tinkering could easily result in over- or underoiled valves.

The consequences of overoiling were unpleasant but not catastrophic: excessive oil consumption and extreme leakage from the valve covers (they all leaked a bit anyway). Even so, it is easy to understand why a customer would be disappointed when his shiny new Knucklehead trailed a thick blue cloud of oil smoke, saturated his legs with oil, or consumed more lubricant than the previous Harleys with total-loss oil systems.

If the adjustment erred on the side of underoiling, the consequences were much more serious, ranging from what *Shop Dope No. 140* described as "squeaking" valves, to rapid and excessive wear of the valves, rockers, shafts, and pushrods.

Even when valve oiling was properly adjusted, the valve-spring covers sometimes overflowed with oil, because with each engine cycle, the vacuum used to pull oil out of the covers sucked debris into the cover to form a sludge that could plug the return lines. As a quick fix, an air fitting was added to the front rocker housing in late 1936, according to *Shop Dope No. 140A,* revised July 20, 1936. Pressurized air applied at the fitting unclogged both scavenge lines. The shop dope also gave instructions to add the air nipple to earlier engines. A more catastrophic consequence of this design flaw saw water entering through the valve arm slot, which could freeze the valve in a block of ice if the temperature dropped below freezing. These problems would not be entirely fixed until 1938, when new covers were introduced that fully enclosed each rocker arm and valve in its own housing.

The two-piece pinion-shaft assembly (through which oil passed to get to the crankpin and connecting rod bearings) was also a cause of excessive oil consumption. Starting with engine number 36EL1755 (and 88 engines with lower serial numbers), a new stub shaft (the part of the pinion-shaft assembly that mounts to the flywheel) was fitted that reduced oil flow to the bottom end, according to *Shop Dope No. 142.* H-D suggested that the new stub shaft be retrofitted in all earlier engines, and the company made it available free of charge on an exchange basis. The shop dope also reiterated that proper adjustment of oil to the rocker arms was critical to making the engine run well and get acceptable oil mileage.

Listed in the shop dope are the eighty-eight earlier engines that were also fitted with the new stub shaft. Interestingly, the list includes *all* engines from 1722–1754, which leads to a question: Why didn't the shop dope say that the modification began with engine number 1722 instead of 1755? Also, the engines listed include six from the first 100 serial numbers (including 1018, ostensibly the eighteenth engine built) and some from each subsequent 100. Why would all of these very early engines still be at the factory when the engines with serial numbers over 1700 were being built? Had the earlier engines been returned for warranty work or had they remained at the factory for working out problems?

1936 PRODUCTION

Just as the start date of 61 production is a mystery, so, too are the ending date and the number of bikes actually produced. As with the start date, I haven't found definitive answers to these questions. I have, however, gathered some information on these topics that I hope will add to the body of knowledge and spark further discussion on the issue.

Consensus among the many leading experts on the 1936 61 is that production began in March or April and ended in July. Information from dealer news bulletins suggests that both of these dates are suspect. As the dealer news bulletins quoted earlier in this chapter suggest, production probably began in early January and quickly ramped up. As winter turned to spring, orders began rolling faster than they could be filled; this is consistent with the prediction printed in the February 24, 1936, dealer news bulletin.

The May 18 issue reassured dealers that "The 61 OHV delivery situation is getting better all the time!" and that production was "getting to a better stride." It went on to predict that, "This is going to be welcome news indeed to our dealers who have been . . . fearful to give this model full selling justice because they were afraid of the delivery situation." Then the bulletin stated that orders could be filled in eight to ten days, and also hinted at what a difficult task it had been to get the new model into production: "To us here at the scene it is nothing short of a miracle the way this factory has handled and brought on production of the new 61." Because the principals are all riding Harleys up in the clouds, we'll never know what actual miracles were worked!

As mentioned previously, the June issue of *The Enthusiast* featured an ad for the 61 OHV. The ad called the 61 the "Sensation of the Motorcycle World" and accurately alluded to its conspicuous lack of promotion: "Minus fanfare and ballyhoo, a new motorcycle has come on the scene and has taken the world by storm." It also featured a photo of Bill Cummings, the winner of the 1934 Indianapolis 500 on his all-white 1936 61. This first official notice about the new model, in Harley's own magazine, came almost six months after the first 61s hit the streets.

The June 15 bulletin stated that orders could be filled in seven to ten days if standard colors and equipment were ordered—more evidence that custom colors were available.

By the deadline for the August 10 issue, delivery time for 61s was up to "about two weeks." This is interesting not so much because it indicates that orders were still coming in as strong at the end of summer as at the beginning, but because it also implies that the 1936 61s were still in production in early August and that the final orders at that time would not be filled until at least mid-August. The bikes discussed in the bulletin were almost certainly 1936 models, since the 1937 models weren't announced to the dealers until the October 19 dealer news bulletin, and not to the public until the November issue of *The Enthusiast*.

A rough timeline can be drawn from the information in these bulletins. Production of 61 demonstrators began no later than mid-January and finished sometime around the middle of February. Production of 61s to fill customer orders began in middle to late February and ended no sooner than mid-August.

How many were built? Production figures compiled by H-D and published in their book, *The Legend Begins*, suggest that 1,704 Knuckleheads were sold in 1936, including 152 Model ES, 1,526 Model ELs, and 26 Model ESs. Consensus among many experts (based on their observation of serial numbers of existing machines) is that nearer 2,000 were built, and this figure is supported by the November 1936 issue of *The Enthusiast*, which boasts that, "In the short time it has been out nearly 2,000 of these sweet jobs have been placed in owners' hands and are rolling up millions of economical miles on American highways." According to Jerry Hatfield, the company's board minutes said 61 sales totaled 1,836 through the end of the business year on September 30, 1936. The highest serial number I have heard of on an existing bike is 2903 (that is, the 1,903rd built).

For some reason, the early machines seem to have survived in greater numbers than the later machines. Gerry Lyons, founder of the 36 EL Registry and editor of the club's newsletter, divided the serial numbers of the 1936 61s known to exist into two lists—those up to 2000 (in other words, the first one thousand 1936 61s built) and those over 2000. In theory, at least, survival rates should have been uniform across the serial number range, resulting in a one-to-one ratio—if two thousand machines really were built. In fact, the ratio is two to one, in favor of the early bikes.

Why would almost twice the percentage of the early bikes survive? I can't think of an *obvious*, logical reason for this circumstance, but there must be one, or else actual production was substantially less than two thousand. Several theories to explain the skewed ratio have been floated in the club's newsletter. Some theorize that whole blocks of late-serialed motorcycles may have been shipped overseas. Others content that H-D skipped blocks of serial numbers to trick rival Indian into thinking the 61 was selling in greater numbers than was actually the case.

I find the first theory plausible. It is not inconceivable that Alfred Rich Child or another foreign franchisee would order fifty to one hundred or more machines at once, all of which probably would have been built as a block, with consecutive serial numbers. According to the book *Harley-Davidson: The Milwaukee Marvel* by Harry Sucher, Child had exclusive sales rights for Japan, Korea, China, and Manchuria and could order machines on open account, with payment not due until 90 days after the shipment reached Japan. Sucher also says that Genijiro Fukui, a representative of Sankyo, "purchased several hundred sidecar outfits from [Child] in 1936" to "fill out their Rikuo line." Sankyo was by this time building the Rikuo, a license-built copy of the H-D VL side-valve Big Twin, so it is unlikely that Sankyo would purchase side-valve sidecar rigs. It is quite possible that many of them were 61s. Similarly, other importers may also have bought large blocks of 61s, all or most of which were probably destroyed or ground up for scrap during World War II.

I find the second theory implausible. Why, when it had just released a motorcycle that set the lead in the big twin market—and one it couldn't build fast enough to keep up with orders—would H-D skip serial numbers just to fool the competition? I don't think they would.

Whatever the actual production figure was—1,704, 1,836, or 2,000—it exceeded H-D's original sales projections. And demand exceeded the factory's production capacity. Clearly, the 61 was a hit. More importantly, the Knucklehead gave H-D a firm technological lead over archrival Indian and their flathead Chief. It also gave them an engine that was in the same technological league as the best European twins. Even though the Depression was far from over in the country at large, the future looked bullish from the boardroom in Milwaukee.

Demand grew for the 61 as the production year went on. The 1936 61s were built into at least late August 1936 (the August 10, 1936, dealer news bulletin specified that delivery time for 61s was "about two weeks"). The bike on the right in the above photo provides a good example of a second-year Knucklehead.

2
PREWAR KNUCKLEHEADS

As nervous as H-D execs may have been about introducing the Knucklehead, they were also confident that the 61's unique combination of style and performance would bring success, despite the remaining flaws in the design. Fortunately, the 61 sold itself, and H-D did a superb job of fixing problems on the fly. Even so, some dealers and

ABOVE: Unlike the pristine trailer queens seen at motorcycle shows today, early customized bikes were built to ride. *Herbert Wagner Collection*

OPPOSITE: The early E models displaced 61 cubic inches. This 1937 EL sports a similar air intake horn as equipped on the 74- and 80-cubic-inch side-valve engines. *David Blattel*

Even the most law-abiding among us (and this group of club presidents shown receiving trophies in 1940 epitomized the law-abiding motorcyclist) has experienced the outlaw impulse at some time or another. *Herbert Wagner Collection*

customers wondered whether they'd been used as unpaid testers, a practice that is now common, especially in the software industry. And, today, we have another term to describe less-than-fully-developed products (as the 1936 61 was at the time it appeared), put onto the market for comment and debugging by favored customers: the "beta" release.

For 1937, H-D's efforts and its customers' patience were rewarded by the introduction of Knucklehead Version 1.1, a much-improved machine that was the product of lessons learned that first year. At the start of its second era, the Knucklehead began to take over. That year, all of the company's models were remade in its image, with revised, dry-sump motors clothed in 61-style finery. With full confidence in its OHV at last, H-D threw back the cloak of silence: the first year's lack of "fanfare and ballyhoo" gave way to a blizzard of promotion in the second, and sales of the 61 began a steady climb that accelerated in the following years. By the end of the decade, the 61 was poised to become Harley's best-selling motorcycle, even though it was also the company's most expensive.

THE 1937 KNUCKLEHEAD

Harley's OHV Big Twin was offered in three versions for 1937: the high-compression 37EL Special Sport Solo, the medium-compression 37E Solo, and the medium-compression 37ES twin with sidecar gearing. All were listed at a retail price of $435. Essential equipment, such as a jiffy stand and steering damper, had to be ordered separately or as part of one of the option groups, at additional cost. A four-speed transmission was standard, but a three-speed transmission could be ordered at no additional cost, or the three-speed-with-reverse transmission could be ordered for $5 extra. Speedster handlebars could be substituted for the standard bars for no extra cost.

Two option groups for solos and one group for sidecar haulers were offered. The Standard Solo Group, which listed for $21.75, included the front safety guard, steering damper, ride control, stoplight and switch, jiffy stand, trip odometer, and front fender light. The Deluxe

In 1937 the new engine received major refinements, helping to harness the potential of the world's first superbike engine.
David Blattel

Although the paint combination shown—black with red stripes edged in gold—was not listed as a standard paint combination, custom color combinations could be ordered; some almost certainly were ordered in this striking combination.

Solo Group included all the items in the standard group and a colored shift knob, foot-pedal rubbers, the Chrome Plate Group, a license plate frame, six-inch round air cleaner, and deluxe saddlebags; it listed for $49. The Standard Group for sidecar or commercial motorcycles, a $20 package, included a front safety guard, a steering damper, a stoplight and switch, ride control, and three-speed transmission with reverse gear.

Other popular individual options offered at the time of order included the air cleaner (in place of the air horn) for $3, the buddy seat for $8.25 (in place of the standard saddle), cadmium-plated rims for $0.50 each, chrome license frame for $0.95, chrome wheel rings for $5, a pair of Little Beauty spotlamps with crossbar for $12.50, deluxe saddlebags for $13.95, a colored dice shifter knob for $0.60, a solo sport windshield for $7, and a stop-light and switch in place of the regular taillight for $3.

Styling Changes

The 1937 models came with a new paint scheme. The art deco gas tank transfer was retained, but for 1937 the transfer was bracketed above and below by thick stripes edged in a complementary color. Gone were 1936's fender panels, replaced by solid-color fenders with stripes matching those on the tank running along each side of each fender's crown. And the 1936 OHV's gorgeous color-matched rims were replaced in 1937 by black-painted rims.

Two regular civilian color combinations were listed in the November 1936 issue of *The Enthusiast*, which introduced the new models for 1937: Bronze Brown striped in Delphine Blue and edged in yellow, and Teak Red striped in black and edged in gold. The brown scheme proved to be unpopular, so a third combination was soon introduced: Delphine Blue striped in Teak Red.

THRILLS
WITH SAFETY

HARLEY-DAVIDSON
MOTORCYCLES

Lots of style—fast get-away—zooming speed—power galore —and a gliding ride that's smooth and trouble-free. Sure thing—these streamlined 1937 Harley-Davidsons are ruggedly built—have perfect balance—instant response of power when driving conditions demand—and dependable brakes both front and rear for quick, easy stops. . . Yes, plenty of thrills— go where you will—get there quickly, safely and economically in the saddle of a 1937 Harley-Davidson. . . See your nearest Harley-Davidson Dealer RIGHT AWAY. Take a FREE ride on a 1937 Harley-Davidson — ask about his Easy Pay Plans. And send in the coupon.

Ride a —

HARLEY-DAVIDSON

HARLEY-DAVIDSON MOTOR CO.
Dept. P, Milwaukee, Wis.
Interested in motorcycling. Send illustrated literature. Postage stamp is enclosed to cover mailing cost.

Name. . . . .
Address. . . . .
My age is ☐ 16-19 years, ☐ 20-30 years,
☐ 31 years and up, ☐ under 16 years.
Check your age group.

Guys and gals outside the Milwaukee Motorcycle Club's clubhouse at Friess Lake, 1934. Backed by both Indian and Harley-Davidson and regulated by the American Motorcycle Association (AMA), the organized club scene exploded in the decade before World War II. *Herbert Wagner Collection*

Police models were offered in Police Silver with black stripes edged in gold.

Of the three regular civilian combinations, the red-and-blue schemes proved to be the overwhelming preference of riders then and restorers now. Viewed from today's perspective on what is clearly an antique machine, the Bronze Brown and Delphine Blue is a handsome combination (see the superbly restored example by Carman Brown in this chapter) that seems suitable for the machine. At the time, though, the brown paint projected a somewhat military or utilitarian image—not at all what most riders wanted on their expensive new sport machine—so it was never popular.

To compensate for the loss of color-matched wheel rims, the 1937 OHV was given a color-matched oil tank in place of the black tank of 1936, resulting in a motorcycle that "is one continuous sweep of color," according to the November 1936 issue of *The Enthusiast*. The new "sweep" of color might have been too much of a good thing: the color-matched oil tanks were discontinued at the end of 1937 and would not be offered again on the H-D Big Twins until the special Hollywood Green paint package offered for the 1955 Panheads.

Engine Updates

Aside from the tendency to spit a bit of oil out the minimal rocker covers, the new OHV mechanism introduced in and refined throughout 1936 proved to be remarkably free of trouble. A weak point in the system was the relatively willowy rocker shaft support arms cast into the cylinder heads. For 1936, two-each support arms had only a partial reinforcement rib that extended barely halfway up the arm, ending far below the level of the rocker shaft holes. The problem with the design only came to light when the bikes were out on the street, revved in friendly competition and fixed by owners and mechanics who had no experience with the new OHV system. During service work, these support arms are easily broken or overstressed if the shaft nuts are cinched up when everything is not correctly aligned or if the thrust washers are left out during assembly.

The solution? The support arms were increased in width and the reinforcing rib on each rocker-shaft support was lengthened, now reaching vertically to the level of the rocker shaft, and the ribs were cast integrally with the cooling fin to the left of the bracket. Other than this change to the support brackets, the heads were unchanged, retaining the cup-type valve-spring covers. This cylinder-head

design is correct for 1937 only. They would be redesigned the following year to solve the other major problem with the OHV's cylinder heads—oil leaking out and dirt and water leaking in through the valve enclosures.

Another chronic source of oil leaks were the cork rocker arm seals in the aluminum rocker housings. Starting with serial number 37E1672, the cork seals were replaced by synthetic-rubber seals. Each of the old-type seals was sandwiched between two steel washers and was held in place by a spring clip. The new seals dispensed with the outer steel washers, the spring clips bearing directly on the rubber seals. While these seals came into regular production on 37E1672, they were also fitted on twenty-eight motors with earlier serial numbers that apparently had not yet been shipped, for whatever reason; these serial numbers are listed in *Shop Dope No. 153*.

The trip odometer version used for 1937 only. A version without the trip odometer was available through 1940.

New for 1937 was the 120-mph speedometer with hash marks at the intermediate 5-mph positions. It was available with or without a trip odometer.

Several updates for 1937 are evident here. Under the footboard is the improved brake rod with clevises at each end. Holes on both the brake pedal and crossover lever were reduced in diameter from 5/16 inch to 1/4 inch for the clevis pins.

That shop dope also instructed dealers to throw away any cork seals in stock and to only use the updated rubber seal on future repairs. The rubber seals listed for $0.15 each.

Just as in 1936, an air horn was standard on the OHV's carburetor, but the 1937 air horn was a new design. The new OHV air horn was a mirror image of the horn on the flathead Big Twins and consisted of a chrome-plated cover and a Parkerized backing plate to attach the cover to the carburetor. The cover is stamped in a rounded, streamlined shape that tapers from front to rear. The 1937-style air horn was standard on OHVs through 1939.

Starting in 1937, an air cleaner was supplied as part of the Deluxe Solo Group, or it could be ordered separately for $3. This air cleaner is the six-inch round air cleaner that had been optional for at least part of 1936. The cover is chrome plated, with the H-D bar-and-shield stamped into its round face and an instruction plate riveted to the rim. The cover is fastened to the backing plate by four screws. The oiled-copper-mesh air cleaner wraps around a mesh support welded to the steel backing plate, which is Parkerized.

The ignition timer was also slightly revised for 1937. The new timer base is like the previous base, except that the notch in the side of the base for the circuit breaker wire is omitted, and the wire attaches to the terminal post below the base. It is routed out of the timer through a hole added to the revised timer housing, into which the base mounts. This new timer base and housing were used through the end of the Knucklehead line in 1947.

About midway through the 1937 production run, the rocker arms were revised to include an oil passage to positively lubricate the pushrod ball socket. Prior to this modification, the pushrod-to-pushrod ball bearing surface was oiled only by scavenge oil pulled from the valve-spring covers by engine vacuum. If the return oil lines from the valve-spring covers were plugged, or if the oil supply to the valves was adjusted down for minimal overspray, the pushrods would be underoiled and wear prematurely. These revised rocker arms were used for the remainder of the 1937 production through early 1939 production (ending with 39EL1902, per *Shop Dope No. 189*), when the rocker arm system was revised so that the oil supply was made nonadjustable.

Early in the year, the brake pedal was cadmium plated, as shown, but later pedals were Parkerized.

Oil tanks were painted the main color of the bike for 1937, so the fuel tank on this example matched the oil tank.

For 1937, the main oil feed line to the oil pump connects to a fitting on the bottom of the tank at the drain hole, rather than at a separate fitting at the back of the tank. While the new fitting configuration may have simplified construction of the oil tank, it made oil changes messier, so it was used for 1937 only.

Note the air nipple on the front rocker housing. This feature had been added in late 1936 and was used again in 1937, since that year's models were fitted with the same cup-type valve spring enclosures that had been used in 1936.

Frame and Fifth Transmission Mount

Like the rest of the 1936 OHV, the bike's double-downtube frame was a radical departure for an H-D street bike. And like the rest of the bike, the frame needed a good bit of tweaking to get it right. Remember, the 61 OHV was originally designed to be a solo sport bike, so Harley-Davidson engineers designed the frame to be as light as possible while still being stiffer and stronger than the single-downtube frames that had been standard for so long on the company's big bikes. Hard use on street and track, and especially under heavy-duty police and sidecar duty, quickly proved that the original design wasn't stout enough for the job. Frames flexed and cracked, and rear brakes chattered. The frame tended to crack under the seat post and at the transmission mount, and the left rear stay sometimes snapped off behind the clutch. To handle these problems, a substantially redesigned frame made its appearance for the second year of 61 OHV production.

Gone were the two continuous downtubes that swept down and back from the steering head to the axle clips. Replacing them were larger-diameter tubes that make the same sweep, but each formed in two sections. The first section on each side connects the steering head to the top of a new drop forging that has integral sidecar mounting loops. The second section connects to the bottom of the sidecar mount forging and sweeps down and back to the axle clips. The new frame is stiffer in torsion, improving handling; it proved much more resistant to cracking than the 1936 frame had been.

The sidecar mount forgings replace the sidecar loops that were brazed or welded onto the continuous downtubes in 1936. The new mounts strengthen the frame and provide a much more durable mounting location for the sidecar.

Exacerbating the problem of the 1936 61's weak frame was the lack of a solid mount between the kickstarter end of the transmission and the frame of all but the very last 1936 61s. Most 1936 61s had an adjustable kick-start-end support consisting of a support bracket that is bolted to the kickstarter cover and a screw adjusted down from the support to contact the frame. A few of

The appearance of H-D's 61 OHV model EL Knucklehead in 1936 set a new standard for high performance, reliability, and near perfect styling.
Herbert Wagner Collection

the last 1936 frames were fitted with a brazed-on clamp bracket that bolted to a revised support bracket bolted to the kickstarter cover to act as an effective fifth mounting point to support the transmission's kickstarter end. The 1937 frame was also fitted with this clamp bracket, and a clamp bracket was fitted to all later Knucklehead frames.

To further strengthen the attachment of the transmission to the frame, the transmission mounts were made stronger, and the transmission mounting plate was twice as thick as that used in 1936. All these modifications helped tremendously, but the problem wasn't really fixed until mid-year, when a new transmission case was introduced with a starter-support boss designed into the casting; this replaced the support bracket bolted to the kickstarter cover. The new transmission case was not replaced until the 1940 model year.

Transmission and Clutch Updates

The starter cover was also modified at about the same time as the revision of the transmission case. Externally, the new cover looks like the previous cover, but inside it has been substantially revised. The machined-in area for the cork seal on the old cover was replaced with a slight recess for the starter-crank washer. The seal was no longer needed because the one-piece crank bushing used with the old cover was replaced by a two-piece bushing with a neoprene seal between the inner and outer length of bushing. Also, the reinforcing ribs around the starter-shaft tunnel were made thicker, and a fifth rib was added.

The new cover continued in production through mid-year 1938. This new cover and bushing, in concert with the fifth transmission mount, made the whole starter

The frame for 1937 was much improved over the 1936 frame, but it also was much heavier. The front downtubes are no longer continuous from a slash-cut single-butted joint below the steering head to the axle clips. Instead, stiffer, straight tubes stretch from the steering head to the new sidecar-mount forgings. Separate tubes run back from the forgings to the axle clips.

After all the problems with frames cracking in 1936, H-D designed a new frame for 1937.

Many of the frame mounts were also made stronger to eliminate the chronic frame-cracking problems experienced with the 1936 Knucklehead frame. This frame also has the mount on the right lower frame tube for the kickstarter side-transmission mount that had been introduced on late 1936 frames.

system stout enough to withstand the vigorous kicking sometimes required to start the OHV.

But it wasn't just the transmission mounts and frame that were prone to breakage under extreme use. On rare occasion, the transmission mainshaft would crack at its clutch-hub end, which meant that, about midway through the production run, a revised transmission mainshaft and mainshaft nut were phased in. The new mainshaft differed from the old one only in that the clutch-hub end of the shaft was increased to ¾ inch in diameter (it had been ¹¹⁄₁₆ inch) and the nut was increased in inside diameter to fit the new shaft. These revisions apparently fixed the problem, because the mainshaft and nut were not revised again until mid-1950, when it was used on the Knucklehead's successor, the Panhead.

The Knucklehead's clutch also suffered when put to use by police departments, especially with the incessant stop-and-go use experienced in traffic control or escort service. Under such use, the driving disc heated up from friction with the outermost fiber disc and conducted the heat to the clutch springs, ruining their temper.

To solve the problem, H-D engineers revised the clutch pack that was incorporated into new machines starting after May 1, according to *Shop Dope No. 166*. The outer fiber disc was replaced by a steel-sprung disc with a new design, and the original "humped" sprung disc was replaced by a plain steel disc. The new sprung disc has eight long, thin, L-shaped slots cut into its outer circumference and notches on its inner circumference to mate with the splines on the driving disc. This disc pack has one fewer fiber discs, one more steel disc, and a redesigned sprung disc. Unfortunately, the revisions to the clutch pack didn't really solve the problem, so the clutch would be redesigned again in mid-1938.

The new taillight had a red lens at the rear and a frosted lens on top to illuminate the license plate, which mounts to a separate bracket. Standard taillight covers were painted the color of the fender, but a chrome-plated cover was included as part of the Chrome Plate Special.

The frame for 1937 was much improved over the 1936 frame, but it also was much heavier. The front downtubes are no longer continuous from a slash-cut single-butted joint below the steering head to the axle clips. Instead, stiffer, straight tubes stretch from the steering head to the new sidecar-mount forgings. Separate tubes run back from the forgings to the axle clips.

Speedo Light Switch and 120-mph Speedometer

The tank-mounted instrument console and speedometer introduced in 1936 became instant classics, so H-D wisely made only minor revisions to them the following year. The instrument panel cover benefited from the addition of a hole just rearward of the ignition switch for the newly added speedometer light switch. This new switch allowed the rider to turn off the speedometer

light independently of the main headlight switch, which extended the life of the bulb and conserved electricity when needed. The new switch's knob is shaped like a tube with a ball on each end, resembling a barbell. The tubular portion is knurled, and the whole knob is cadmium plated. This style of knob was used only for 1937 and 1938.

All 1937 instrument panel covers had a hole on the right side for the trip odometer reset shaft, whether or

These fender stripes replaced the fender panels used in 1936.

Standard wheel rims for 1937 were painted black, but cadmium-plated rims were available for $0.50 each; bolt-on chrome wheel rings were available for $5.00.

Note that the rear mount for the chain guard is now part of the fender stay clip, rather than the 1936-only separate bracket riveted to the front fender stay.

PREWAR KNUCKLEHEADS

73

not the motorcycle was fitted with a tripmeter-equipped speedometer. The hole for the reset was sealed with a rubber grommet that had an opening for the reset rod, if one was fitted.

In a somewhat optimistic move—but one in keeping with the sporting image of the machine—a new, 120-mph face was added to tripmeter and non-tripmeter speedometers for 1937. The styling of these speedometers is like the styling of the 100-mph speedometers of 1936, except that the numerals 110 and 120 were added. A speedometer without a tripmeter was standard, but a speedometer *with* tripmeter was fitted if either of the two option groups was ordered, or it could be ordered in place of the standard speedometer for $3. The 120-mph speedometer with 5-mph hash marks and a tripmeter was used only for 1937, but the same speedo without a tripmeter was used from 1937 through 1940.

Joe Petrali was larger than life, and he piloted this streamlined EL-powered racer to a new speed record of 136 miles per hour in 1937 at Daytona Beach, Florida. *Doug Mitchel*

HARLEY-DAVIDSON

ABOVE: Like the brake pedal, the clutch pedal was cadmium plated for at least part of the 1937 production year. Later pedals were Parkerized.

LEFT: The far bike wears what Harley-Davidson hoped would be its signature paint combination for 1937—Bronze Brown with Delphine Blue striping edged in gold. To popularize its new models, Harley-Davidson printed up a two-color brochure with the new color, touting the beautiful appearance it gave to the 1937 machines.

The trip odometer was not included in the Standard Group for sidecar or commercial motorcycles, though some 1937 OHVs were equipped with non-tripmeter speedometers. On these speedometers, the odometer has six numeral wheels, rather than the five that are on the tripmeter speedos. The sixth numeral wheel records tenths of a mile, and the tenth numerals are red on a white background. This speedometer, with 5-mph hash marks, is the correct non-tripmeter speedo for 1937–1940. The speedometer with trip odometer could be ordered in place of the standard speedometer on these machines for $3.

ABOVE: Black wheels became standard as of 1937.

RIGHT: Many of the frame mounts were also made stronger to eliminate the chronic frame-cracking problems experienced with the 1936 Knucklehead frame.

Competition

In its second year, the 61 OHV began to make its way into the winner's circle and into the record books. On March 13, 1937, Joe Petrali piloted a specially prepared 61 to a new AMA straightaway record of 136.183 mph. On April 8, a true iron man named Fred Ham took a day off from his job as a motorcycle cop to try breaking the world record for the number of miles ridden in 24 hours on a stock 61 that he had purchased in October 1936—and he planned to do all the riding himself. With the help of a crew of over twenty, oil flares to mark the course at night, and quarts of cold milk to keep him alert, Ham rode 1,825 miles, an average of 76.6 mph, and also broke 44 other intermediate records. On May 16, Al Aunapa

Given the EL's superior performance over the flathead-powered Harleys, police gravitated quickly to the overhead-valve engine package for pursuing the bad guys on the highway. *Doug Mitchel*

The 1937 Knucklehead was a vastly improved machine compared to the 1936 original. Aesthetically, though, it lost ground.

rode his 61 to victory in the 100-mile TT National Championship. In addition, 61s were ridden to dozens of other victories on tracks and hills around the world.

1937 Production

The 61 OHV found even wider acceptance in its second year, as did the flathead 45s and Big Twins that were given the OHV's styling for 1937. Overall, H-D's sales rose by a satisfying 19 percent. Of the 11,674 Harleys built that year, 2,205 were 61s. This total includes 126 E, 1,829 EL, and 70 ES. The following year would bring further improvement to the Knucklehead, at last curing the problem that had contributed so much to its delayed introduction and had given owners of 1936 and 1937 Knuckleheads such fits: oil leaks from the valve gear.

THE 1938 KNUCKLEHEAD

As the October 1937 issue of *The Enthusiast* noted, the changes for 1938 were an "inside story" whose main theme was "smoother, quieter, cleaner." And, as we shall see, these were apt descriptions of the updated model.

The OHV Big Twin model line was pared down to just two offerings for 1938: the high-compression 38EL Special Sport Solo and the medium-compression 38ES twin with sidecar gearing. Accordingly, all non-police solo models should be marked 38EL and all non police bikes marked 38E (remember, the S in ES was not marked on the crankcase as part of the serial number) should be sidecar or commercial machines. Most police solo models were probably 38Es, however, and some civilian solo 38Es were probably special ordered,

ABOVE: The chrome-plated chain-inspection cover was standard for 1936 and 1937 also. Starting in 1938, it was painted black.

BELOW: For 1938, the rear brake was again substantially modified. The backing plate was given a larger reinforcement plate, and the shoe pivot was replaced with a cup bearing that clamped both shoes together at the rear.

Wide riding belts, breeches, high boots, peaked caps, and H-D wings marked the motorcycle look of the 1930s. Pictured left to right are Gary Koep, Leo Duffren, and Al Sharon at a Shawano rally in the 1930s. *Herbert Wagner Collection*

so solo models marked 38E were undoubtedly built in this period.

Both the EL and ES were fitted with the high-domed, high-compression pistons for 1938 because the low-domed, medium-compression pistons had been discontinued at the end of the 1937 model year. The ES was given a lower compression ratio by fitting a compression plate underneath each cylinder. Gearing for the two models was unchanged.

All models were listed at a retail price of $435 (the same price as in 1937), but, for the first time, they had to be ordered with one of the option groups, at additional cost. A four-speed transmission was standard, but a three-speed transmission could be specified at the time of order for no additional cost. For an extra $5,

the three-speed-with-reverse transmission could be ordered. Speedster handlebars could be substituted for the standard bars at no extra cost.

Two option groups for solos and one group for sidecar haulers were offered. The Standard Solo Group included the front safety guard, steering damper, stoplight and switch, jiffy stand, trip odometer, and front fender light; this configuration was listed for $16.70 (which was about $5 cheaper than in 1937, probably because the ride control was no longer part of the package). The $49.75 Deluxe Solo Group included all the items in the standard group plus four-ply tires, ride control, a colored shift knob, the six-inch round air cleaner, Deluxe Saddlebags, and the Chrome Plate Special (includes chrome-plated handlebars, headlamp, instrument panel, wheel rings,

"You Can't Beat *Fun*"
and the World's Greatest Fun is Riding a
HARLEY-DAVIDSON

Harley-Davidson

HARLEY-DAVIDSON
Enthusiast

See your Harley-Davidson dealer. Get "hep" to the big times and wonderful companionship in store for you when you ride this world's champion motorcycle. Learn about the fun-packed activities of the local motorcycle club. Take a ride on a snappy new 1938 model—ask about Easy Payment Plan. *Send in the coupon now!*

HARLEY-DAVIDSON MOTOR CO., Dept. P, Milwaukee, Wis.
   Motorcycling sounds like great sport to me. Send illustrated literature and FREE motorcycling magazine, "The Enthusiast." No obligation. Postage stamp is enclosed to cover mailing cost.

Name...

Address...
   My age is ( ) 16-19 years, ( ) 20-30 years, ( )31 years and up, ( ) under 16 years. Check your age group.

When writing to advertisers please mention Popular Mechanics

The upper and lower valve covers of the 1938 model were fastened together by roundhead screws with threaded screw plates below, rather than with the individual nuts shown here.

For 1938, the frame and forks were also made stouter for a better-handling machine.

Another styling change for 1938 was the new striping on the tank. Rather than running stripes above and below the tank transfers, the 1938 machines had a single stripe on each tank, extending forward and back from the tank transfers.

Another styling change for 1938 was the new striping on the tank. Rather than running stripes above and below the tank transfers, the 1938 machines had a single stripe on each tank, extending forward and back from the tank transfers.

parking lights, fender strips, and license plate frame). The Standard Group for sidecar or commercial motorcycles, a $14.25 package, included a front safety guard, a steering damper, a stoplight and switch, and ride control. (Note that the three-speed transmission with reverse gear was no longer part of the package.)

Other popular individual options included the air cleaner for $5, the buddy seat for $8.25 (in place of the standard saddle), cadmium-plated rims for $0.50 each, chrome license frame for $0.95, the Chrome Plate Special for $15.50, a pair of Little Beauty spotlamps with crossbar for $13.25, deluxe saddlebags for $15.50, a colored dice shifter knob for $0.65, a solo sport windshield for $7, and—making its debut on the order blank—a rear safety guard for $5.50.

Color Harmony

The standard paint scheme was revised for the new model year. Once again, the art deco gas tank transfer was retained, and the gas tanks and fenders were painted in a solid color without panels. For 1938, though, a thin stripe outlined in a complementary color runs down the centerline of the tank sides and aft of the tank transfer. A similar stripe curves along the top of the fender skirt, much further down the sides of the fenders than the stripes used in the previous year. And the oil tank was painted black for 1938, reversing the change to a color-matched tank that had been made in 1937.

Standard 1938 paint colors were Teak Red with black stripes edged in gold, Venetian Blue with white stripes edged in Burnt Orange, Hollywood Green with gold stripes edged in black, and Silver Tan with Sunshine Blue stripes. Police models were painted silver with black stripes.

Color harmony was the stated goal of some plating changes for 1938. "Chrome parts which only dazzled and did not carry out the color harmony of the machine were eliminated," according to an ad in the October 1937 issue of *The Enthusiast*. The ad went on to specify that

By the time this 1938 model had been built, the EL had already established a land-speed record of 136.185 miles per hour.
David Blattel

the timer cover was now plated in cadmium rather than chrome, and the "[c]hain inspection cover on all models is now black and adds to the color harmony of the lower part of the machine." Cadmium plating was also eliminated. According to the ad, "as soon as possible all nuts and bolts will be Parkerized instead of cadmium plated."

Fully Enclosed Rockers and Valves

Even when the adjustable rocker-oiling system was properly adjusted on the 1936 and 1937 machines, a fine mist of oil was continually vented out the rocker arm opening in the valve-spring enclosure. Nothing serious, but it was irritating nonetheless. As an ad in the October 1937 issue of *The Enthusiast* said, "Oil seepage resulting in dirty motors and making for soiled clothing has been an evil that has been the source of much complaint in the past. With the growing popularity of light-colored riding clothing, especially club uniforms, the need for clean motors is self-evident."

More troublesome was the potential for oil spray to leak out, which meant that dirt and water could leak in and quickly ruin valves and guides—not to mention the rockers and shafts, which were almost completely exposed to the elements. Worse yet, the dirt didn't just leak in: it was actually sucked in by the engine vacuum that was used to scavenge oil from the valve spring enclosure. This dirt was then ingested into the engine along with the scavenged oil.

After two full years of complaints and warranty repairs, H-D chose to fix the problem once and for all, introducing truly effective full enclosures for the rocker arms and valves for 1938. One of these new enclosure assemblies was used for each valve, and each assembly consisted of a lower cover, a cover cap, a gasket, two screw plates, and screws.

The lower cover was a curiously shaped stamping with a lower cup that enclosed the valve stem and spring. It included an oil-scavenge line attached to the right side of the cup, a "trough" that extended to the right to hold the rocker seal in place and cover the lower half of the rocker and shaft, a small hole to vent the cover, and a completely open top area. A flange on the valve guide

The instrument panel shows the new "idiot" lights that replaced the ammeter and mechanical oil pressure indicator in 1938. The left indicator (voltage) has a green lens, and the right indicator (oil pressure) has a red lens. The skullface panel with the colored lenses is correct for 1938 only.

fastened the lower cover to the cylinder head, and an asbestos gasket was sandwiched between the cover and the cylinder head.

A separate cap completed the valve enclosure, covering the top of the pocket and the trough. The cap-to-cover junction was sealed by a gasket, then fastened together by screws that were inserted through holes in the cap, gasket, and lower cover and cinched tight into threaded holes in two separate screw plates for each enclosure.

The oil lines from the lower cover were larger in diameter than the lines used the previous year (to reduce the tendency for them to clog) and attached to larger-diameter fittings on the rocker boss. The small vent hole allowed air to enter the enclosure when engine vacuum scavenged oil from the lower cover. Its location on the lower cover prevented water from dripping in, and its small size kept dirt ingestion to an acceptable minimum.

The new enclosures were a welcome improvement over the old type. Oil consumption decreased and the bike stayed cleaner, inside and out. The updates worked so well that the enclosure stampings remained unchanged through 1947. (Notably, though, the screws and screw plates were updated in 1939.) Rocker enclosures were painted black.

H-D even offered a kit to retrofit the new enclosures to 1936–1937 cylinder heads, and most of the older machines that exist today have these enclosures. *Shop Dope No. 172* gave instructions for the retrofit, and even mentioned that the factory would perform the work if the heads were returned to Milwaukee.

Cylinder head cooling fins on the new castings were relieved to allow clearance for the enclosures, but were otherwise unchanged on early through mid-1938 machines. Later in the 1938 production run, the cylinder-head castings were again modified, this time to further stiffen the rocker arm supports on the left side of the castings and provide more clearance for the rocker covers. The revised supports still joined in the center to form a V, but the V now had a flat atop each branch of the V, running from the reinforcing rib on the inside of the V to its rounded outside tip. The rocker shaft holes were no longer on the centerline of each ear of the V; rather, they were to the outside of the centerline, centered on the radius of the outer rounded tip. Head castings with the new rocker supports and drilled primer cup bosses were used only on later 1938 machines.

Because the new rocker enclosures also held the rocker arm seal in place in the aluminum rocker housing, the snap ring that held the seal in place on 1936–1937 motors was no longer needed. Consequently, both the front and rear rocker housings were revised to omit the groove that held the snap ring in place.

And the new rocker covers were so efficient at keeping out dirt and water that the oil scavenge lines from the covers were no longer prone to clogging up with oil-dirt-water sludge, so the new front head rocker housing was further revised to omit the air nipple that had been added in mid-1936. The rear head's rocker housing was fitted with an adapter for its exhaust valve's rocker enclosure. Rocker housings with these revisions were used through mid-1939.

The final top-end update for 1938 was to the exhaust valve's lower spring collar. The 1936 through early 1938 collar with an inside diameter of $2\frac{1}{32}$ inch was replaced in mid-1938 by the same lower spring collar (with an inside diameter of $\frac{27}{32}$ inch) used on the intake valve.

Only a minor update was made to the engine's lower end, and it, too, continued the themes of "smoother, quieter." In a move to make their timing gears rounder and the teeth more precisely shaped, H-D purchased a new machine that shaved the gears to their final shape with greater precision, reducing runout and "high spots," which the company claimed reduced operating noise and made the engine's overall operation smoother.

Oiling System Updates

Another common source of oil leakage were the banjo-type oil fittings that secured the oil lines to the oil tank, especially the under-tank oil feed line fitting that was integral with the drain valve on the 1937 models. Continuing the theme of "cleaner" for 1938, H-D moved the oil feed line fitting to the back of the oil tank's right side and changed the oil tank's oil line fittings to compression-type fittings that offered better sealing. This new tank is correct for 1938 and 1939 and is again painted black. Of course, the oil line fittings were also updated for the compression-type connections.

To improve breather action and help prevent clogging of the breather line in cold weather, the vent line from the oil tank to the crankcase was increased in size from $\frac{1}{4}$ inch to $\frac{3}{8}$ inch.

The oil pump was updated for use with the diaphragm-type oil pressure switch introduced with the new oil pressure indicator light housed in the instrument cover. The major pump modification involved lengthening the boss surrounding the sensing hole to allow clearance for the switch. This style of oil pump was used

Fully enclosed valves greeted customers of the 1938 EL. Prior to that, the new OHV engine had partially exposed rocker arms that spattered oil onto the rider's legs. *Doug Mitchel*

Note the arrowheads at the front of the pinstripes on the front fender of this 1938 California Highway Patrol bike.

only for 1938. The switch breaks the oil pressure indicator light circuit when the oil pressure reaches 3 psi, shutting off the indicator light. This switch threads into an adapter, which threads into the oil-pressure-sensing-hole boss on the oil pump. The switch is correct for 1938–1947, but this specific adapter was used on the OHV models for 1938 (but also on later side-valve models).

Stiffer Frame

The new, stronger frame that had been introduced in 1937 was a vast improvement over 1936's willowy frame, but the 1937 frame still exhibited signs of flexing when ridden at its limits or when lugging a sidecar. And its relatively lightweight rear frame tubes and open slot on the left axle clip's brake stay were also thought to contribute to rear brake chatter.

For 1938, H-D fitted their Big Twins with a revised frame that was markedly stouter than its predecessors. Reinforcements made this year include a frame strut that triangulates the frame between the backbone tube and the lower part of the steering-head forging made of larger-diameter tubing (1 inch instead of $7/8$ inch); rear tubes that connect the axle clip forgings to the front portion of the frame made of heavier-gauge steel (14-gauge instead of 16-gauge); seat post braces made of heavier-gauge steel

and ½ inch wider; a transmission-mounting bracket and rear support made of heavier-gauge steel; and a brake stay on the left axle clip with a cap brazed on to close the end of the stay slot.

The frame's steering head was also improved with the addition of a lower self-aligning head cone that has a convex base. According to the writeup in *The Enthusiast* that introduced the new models, the convex base allows it to "shift into alignment no matter how tight the bearing may be; bearing pitting is eliminated and the bearing race is free to travel all around. They'll now retain their easy-handling qualities for life." Over the 1938 production run, the forging hallmarks on the left side of the steering head were phased out, and all subsequent Knucklehead steering heads lacked these marks.

The frame's toolbox strap was also revised for 1938—not to make it stiffer, but to make it easier and cheaper to manufacture. On the previous frame, the mounting bolts for the toolbox were each inserted through a hole in the toolbox strap and threaded into holes in the rectangular plates spot welded to the wheel side of the strap. On the 1938 frame, the spot-welded plates were replaced by swaged-on threaded fittings. These fittings were used on all subsequent frames.

Sometime during 1938 production, the frame was improved yet again when a new left axle-clip forging was phased into production. The new forging no longer needed the brazed-on cap to close the end of the open slot for the brake stay because the slot's end was not left open on the new forging. Left-axle clip forgings with closed brake stay slots were used on all subsequent Knucklehead frames.

Revised Instrument Panel and Speedometer

Long before 1938, car and motorcycle manufacturers had begun to realize that, by making their machines more sophisticated and easier to operate, they could make them appeal to a new group of buyers who were not necessarily interested in, or knowledgeable about, mechanics. These buyers weren't interested in tinkering with their machine—they just wanted reliable transport. To these new customers, finicky features such as

Standard colors for 1938 were Teak Red with black striping, Venetian Blue with white striping, Hollywood Green with gold striping, Silver Tan with Sunshine Blue Striping, and Police Silver with black striping.

ammeters and adjustable oiling for the valve gear were unnecessary anachronisms that at best only confused them with more information than they knew what to do with—and at worst were like an open mineshaft that lay in wait to trap them.

Anticipating the next stage of this trend—but years ahead of standard practice in the automotive industry—H-D made an unpopular but wise move in 1938 when it abandoned the ammeter and mechanical oil pressure indicator in favor of what are today called "idiot lights."

The ammeter was an elegant device that had been a popular feature because it provided useful information about the condition of the motorcycle's charging system. Why would H-D risk alienating their customers by deleting it and the marginally useful but charming mechanical oil indicator? The most important reason was probably cost—the two gauges were far more expensive to manufacture

than were indicator lights—but the new system brought with it some very real benefits: reduced complexity and vulnerability of the oiling and electrical systems.

The mechanical oil pressure indicator had required a steel oil line that connected to the oil pump and was routed along the frame to the gauge. This routing protected the line well, but the potential was there for vibration to cause the line to crack or to abrade through, or for the connections to leak, with potentially catastrophic results for the engine. The new oil pressure indicator light used a sensor switch on the oil pump and a wire to the indicator light. When oil pressure drops below 3 psi, the switch closes the circuit, lighting the indicator lamp and illuminating the red lens that covers the opening on the right, where the mechanical indicator was formerly mounted.

Similarly, the entire current of the electrical system had to be routed through the ammeter for it to operate. Again, the added wiring was well protected, but Murphy's Law sometimes wins out even over slim odds. Instead of current, the new indicator light responds to the voltage difference between the battery and the new third terminal on the generator cutout relay. When battery voltage is higher than generator voltage, current flows through the lamp and illuminates the green lens in the opening formerly occupied by the ammeter. When generator voltage reaches battery voltage, the light goes out. According to an ad in the October 1937 issue of *The Motorcyclist*, "The [instrument panel] lights are distinctly arresting, even in the daytime."

In addition to the new indicator lights, the 1938 instrument panel cover was given two other noteworthy modifications: the tripmeter reset hole was replaced by a slot, and a ⅜-inch hole was added on the left side for a police speedometer hand lock.

The new tripmeter-reset slot is covered by a solid (for non-tripmeter models) or cutout (for tripmeter models) metal cover that is attached by two screws. The hand lock hole is sealed by a clip-on cover on civilian models. The wiring underneath the cover was revised for the new indicator lights, and the horn and light switch wiring were rerouted between handlebar switches and the instrument panel to eliminate chafing. The instrument cover was painted black on motorcycles ordered with the standard option groups, or chrome-plated on motorcycles ordered with the Deluxe Solo Group or the Chrome Plate Special (which also included chrome-plated handlebars, wheel rings, parking lights, fender strips, and license plate frame).

The standard speedometer on the Knucklehead for 1938 was equipped with a tripmeter (based on the fact that all models had to be ordered with one of the option groups and all the option groups for the Knucklehead included the trip odometer). This speedometer looks like the earlier speedometer, except that hash marks were added for the 2-mph intervals between the numerals, which are spaced at 10-mph intervals between 10 and 120. These new hash marks replaced the 5-mph hash marks formerly used. This new speedometer is correct for 1938–1940 61s.

Some 61s may have been fitted with non-tripmeter speedometers. If so, they were equipped with the old-style speedometer with 5-mph hash marks because the speedometer with 2-mph hash marks was made only with the tripmeter.

Transmission and Clutch

At the start of the 1938 model year, a number of small, largely invisible changes were made to the Knucklehead transmission and clutch. These included a new starter cover; a larger, stronger clutch release finger and revised finger stud with a longer bushing; a higher oil-level communicating hole between the starter cover and the gear case (to keep foreign particles from entering the gear case); reinforced mainshaft second gear ("fully 75 percent" stronger, according to an ad in the October 1937 issue of *The Motorcyclist*); wider lugs on the second-gear shifter clutch; wider lugs and beveled engaging surfaces on the fourth-gear shifter clutch; and a third-gear engaging clutch with more clearance from the side of the lugs. Externally, a revised clutch-operating lever and a revised clutch pedal spring were also introduced. The release lever is like the previous lever, except that the left end has only one slot (instead of two), and the two pieces of the lever are welded together (rather than being brazed). This lever is Parkerized. The 1938 clutch pedal springs were like the previous springs, except that they have only nineteen coils (versus twenty-two). These springs are painted black.

Most of the aforementioned changes were inconsequential in and of themselves, but they were necessary to implement a series of midyear changes that would constitute yet another attempt to fix two nagging problems with the Big Twin clutch: overheating and a weak throwout bearing.

To make the clutch more resistant to overheating under police use, the clutch was given a new disc pack, an asbestos insulating gasket for the driving disc, a revised hub locknut, and new clutch springs. These parts were fitted to new machines after February 1, 1938, according to *Shop Dope No. 175*.

The new clutch disc pack used two lined steel discs, two plain steel discs, one notched fiber disc, and one sprung disc. The plain steel and notched fiber discs were the same type that had been used on previous clutches, but the lined discs and spring disc were new parts. Each lined disc consisted of a steel disc with notches around the outer circumference (to mate with the splines on the clutch drum) and fiber linings riveted onto each side of the disc. The new spring disc still has the L-slots on its outer circumference but lacks the spline notches on its inner circumference. This new disc pack was used through the 1940 model year, after which an all-new clutch made its debut.

Shorter, stiffer, and wound of thicker wire, the new clutch springs were protected from clutch heat by the new asbestos gasket, installed between the new clutch springs and the driving plate. Also added in this update were a longer clutch-hub locknut and a longer adjusting screw. All these parts were used through the 1940 model year.

The second big change introduced the second update to the throwout bearing and a revised clutch pushrod for the new bearing. Curiously, the new pushrod was first fitted to new machines more than two weeks before the new bearing (after February 25, 1938, for the pushrod and after March 8, 1938, for the bearing, according to *Shop Dope No. 174*). The 8-ball clutch throwout bearing that had been used on Knuckleheads since late 1936 was replaced by a 10-ball throwout bearing that was less prone to seizing. In the shop dope, dealers were instructed to retrofit any unsold machines with the new bearing and pushrod and to return for exchange any of these parts replaced under warranty.

This throwout bearing was much larger and stouter than the previous bearing, but it still wasn't good enough and would be replaced the following year. Consequently, late in the 1938 production run, the starter cover was revised yet again, this time to include a reinforcing rib between the filler hole and the boss for the clutch-release-shaft opening—and for added clearance for the 25-ball clutch throwout bearing that replaced the 10-ball throwout bearing.

Finally, a new clutch pedal and bracket were introduced in midyear. The new clutch pedal is taller in height (5.75 inches versus 4.25 inches) but shorter in length (9 inches versus 9.125 inches) than the previous pedal; it, too, was only used for the latter part of 1938. The new clutch pedal bracket is like the previous bracket, except

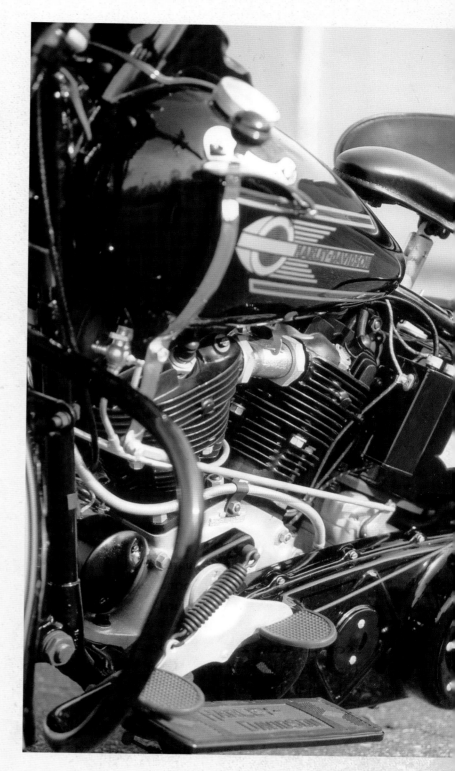

For 1939, Harley-Davidson introduced a new set of transmissions with a sliding gear first (in three-speed and three-speed-with-reverse transmissions) or second (in four-speeds).

Another new instrument panel was introduced in 1939. The new panel was nicknamed the "cat's eye" because of the almond-shaped windows for the generator and oil warning lights. Shadows highlight the V-shaped ridge that ends just aft of the restyled speedometer light knob, also new for 1939. Although the cat's-eye cover was used through 1946, this V is only apparent on covers through model year 1942.

that it is taller (9.75 inches versus 8¹⁵⁄₁₆ inches) and has four 0.75-inch holes in a square pattern on the bracket midsection instead of the former bracket's two holes. This bracket was used again for 1939.

Forks and Handlebars

The 1938 forks were formed from stronger tubing to make them less prone to flexing. The fork was also fitted with wider front fender mounting tabs to make the tabs even more resistant to cracking from vibration. Characterized by larger tubing and old-style spring perches with the grease fittings on the front part of the spring perches (rather than on the sides), these forks were used only in 1938.

Also for 1938, the bend on the handlebars was revised to allow more clearance for the rider's legs when the bars are turned. These bars are correct for 1938 through to mid-1946. The individual bars are brazed to the cast

center section on 1938 through mid-1945 Buckhorn bars and on 1938–1942 Speedster bars; the bars are welded to the center section on late 1945 to mid-1946 Buckhorn bars and 1943 to mid-1946 Standard bars. Bars are painted black.

Police Bike Updates

Police bikes were given two new major convenience features for 1938. The first and most important was the magnetic speedometer hand stop available for mounting on the handlebar. With this new device, an officer could pace a car and press a button to freeze the speedometer needle at the pace speed. The second was a streamlined, polished-aluminum siren.

The steady increase in electric-powered police accessories, especially radios, was the impetus for the introduction of a new high-output police generator in mid-1938. The Model 32E2R had longer armatures and fields to produce more current than the standard Model 32E generator. The new generator is a six-volt, two-brush generator that is used with a voltage regulator instead of with a cutout relay.

Mature Design

After the hundreds of running changes implemented in 1936 and 1937, the design of the Knucklehead stabilized somewhat starting in 1938, as many of the modifications introduced that year fixed nagging problems well enough that they would not be changed again during Knucklehead production. And, for the first time the Knucklehead design lived up to its early promise. From 1938 on, improved brakes, the use of indicator lights, and the finish on many of the parts (cadmium-plated speedometer cable housings and Parkerized brake foot pedal are two examples) remained unchanged—except on the rare wartime bikes—through the end of Knucklehead production in 1947.

1938 Production

After the 20 percent rise in sales that had so pleased H-D in 1937, the 1938 sales were a big disappointment. Overall sales declined 30 percent—the result of flagging interest in the 45s, 74s, and 80s as the excitement initiated by their restyling in 1937 dissipated. The one ray of hope was that the 61 was even more popular, its sales rising more than 20 percent to 2,478. Of this total, 2,289 were ELs and 189 were ESs. The 61s accounted for about 30 percent of overall Harley sales (up from 15 percent the year before), and this trend would continue in the following years.

THE 1939 KNUCKLEHEAD

The OHV Big Twin model line for 1939 included only the high-compression 39EL Special Sport Solo and the medium-compression 39ES twin with sidecar gearing. In addition, a special police package was offered, combining the medium-compression motor, the three-speed transmission, and medium gearing. All models were listed at a retail price of $435 (the same price as in 1937 and 1938) and had to be ordered with

The fender stripes in the 1938 machine were moved down to the top edge of the valance.

one of the option groups, at additional cost. A four-speed transmission was standard, but a three-speed transmission could be specified at the time of order for no additional cost. For $5 extra, the three-speed-with-reverse transmission could be ordered. Speedster handlebars could be substituted for the standard bars for no extra cost.

Offerings included two option groups for solos and one group for sidecar haulers. The Standard Solo Group included the front safety guard, steering damper, stoplight and switch, jiffy stand, trip odometer, front fender light and four-ply tires; the package listed for $15.50. The Deluxe Solo Group for 1939 was expanded, and included all the items in the standard group, ride control, a colored shift knob, the six-inch round air cleaner, deluxe saddlebags, deluxe solo saddle, and the Chrome Plate Special (which included chrome-plated handlebars,

Improvements, rather than innovations, earmark the overhead-valve Big Twin for 1939. Among the EL's improvements were modified clutch and transmission designs for smoother shifting. *Doug Mitchel*

The 1939 models came closer to recapturing the sporty styling of the original Knuckleheads than did any other year. Note that the patent decal was moved back to the toolbox cover for 1939, where it had been in 1936.

This stunning 1939 EL features solid wheels, made by Wolf Wheel Company of Akron, Ohio. These are period accessories that have been on the bike since it was new, according to Reg Shanks, the Vancouver Island, British Columbia, dealer who originally sold the bike in 1939.

headlamp, instrument panel, taillight cover, relay cover, exhaust pipe covers, license-plate frame fender strips, and stainless-steel top fender strips); it listed for $47. The Standard Group for sidecar or commercial motorcycles listed for $14 and included a front safety guard, a steering damper, a stoplight and switch, trip odometer, fender light, and four-ply tires. It is interesting to note that the three-speed transmission with reverse gear was no longer included in the package.

Other popular individual options included the air cleaner for $3, the plain buddy seat for $8.25 (in place of the standard saddle), the deluxe buddy seat for $10.50 (in place of the standard saddle), chrome license frame for $0.95, the Chrome Plate Special for $13.50, deluxe saddlebags for $13.95, a solo sport windshield for $6.50, and—making its debut on the order blank—chrome exhaust pipe covers for $1.75.

Styling Changes

Changes for 1939 took Knucklehead styling to heights it hadn't reached since 1936—and it would never reach this level again. Elements of the new style that made it so stunning included the new paint scheme, streamlined "cat's-eye" instrument panel, "boattail" taillight, and new stainless-steel fender trim.

New Paint

With the possible exception of the one used in 1936, the paint scheme introduced for 1939 is probably the handsomest ever employed on an H-D Big Twin. Like the 1936 scheme, the 1939 paint scheme was again two-tone, but this time the contrasting panels were on sides of the gas tanks, rather than on the fenders. From a side view, the top edge of the panel continues the long diagonal line of the frame, from the steering head to the axle clips. From a front view, the top lines of the panels are seen to curve downward and toward the center of the bike in a V shape. A pinstripe accentuates the curved top line of the panel. The art deco tank transfer was used for the last time with the new tank panels.

Standard paint colors for 1939 were Airway Blue with white panels, black with ivory panels, and Teak

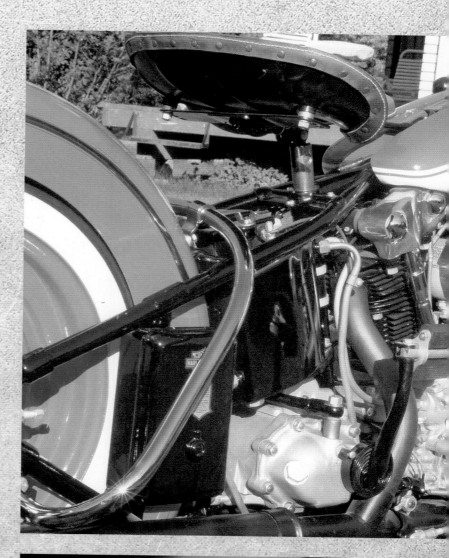

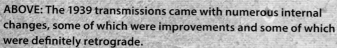

ABOVE: The 1939 transmissions came with numerous internal changes, some of which were improvements and some of which were definitely retrograde.

ABOVE RIGHT: Among the improvements for 1939 was yet another throwout bearing (the fourth in four years), shown in this photo as the truncated, cone-shaped part inside the kickstarter cover.

RIGHT: On the four-speed gate, neutral was placed between second and third gear. The new transmissions were unpopular because the rider had to go through the nonsynchromesh second gear every time he shifted from neutral to first (on four-speeds), or through the nonsynchromesh first every time he shifted to reverse (three-speed-with-reverse). This shifter gate for a three-speed-with-reverse transmission is on a 1939 EL.

This 1939 EL boasts added chromed parts and a two-person buddy seat. *Doug Mitchel*

In addition to the black-with-ivory-panels scheme shown on this bike, standard colors included Airway Blue with white panels, Teak Red with black panels, and Police Silver with black striping.

Red with black panels. Police models were available in Police Silver with black stripes.

Cat's-Eye Instrument Cover

A restyled instrument cover added to the impact of the new tank panels. This new cover is longer and more streamlined than the previous cover and has a pronounced V-shaped ridge aft of the ignition switch hole. The rectangular apertures for the warning lights were replaced by cat's-eye-shaped openings, giving rise to the nickname of this dash. Lenses over these openings were green and red.

Also restyled was the speedometer light switch knob at the rear of the instrument panel. The 1937–1938 bar-bell-shaped knob was replaced by a disc-shaped knob, slightly rounded on top, with a knurled edge; it was cadmium plated. This instrument panel and speedo light knob are correct for 1939–1942.

Rather than being painted black or chrome plated like previous covers had been, the 1939 cover was painted to match the color of the tank top and fenders, adding further to the distinctive new look. As the September 1938 issue of *The Enthusiast* bragged: "From front to rear there is a continuous flow of color!" Chrome-plated instrument panels were optional.

ABOVE: Harley introduced the new "boattail" taillight for 1939.

RIGHT: Obviously, the springs should not be chromed, but this photo does show two subtle new features of the 1939 and later machines: the grease fitting sticking out to each side of the rigid leg's spring perch, and the larger oiler on the front brake coil (shown just above the top nut of the forks).

This machine sports the accessory spotlamps, stainless-steel trim strips for the top of the fenders (included in the Chrome Plate Special), and rear safety guard.

"Boattail" Taillight

For 1939, the small "beehive" taillight was replaced by a larger, more streamlined assembly. It was dubbed the "boattail" because its shape evoked the image of the streamlined rear ends used on the muscle boats of the era. Standard taillight bodies were painted the color of the fenders, but chrome-plated bodies were available. This taillight is correct for 1939–1941 (in 1942 the taillight unit was only slightly revised).

The rear fender was revised for 1939 to omit the taillight shroud that had been necessary for the old-style taillight, and to add mounting holes for the new taillight and stainless-steel trim pieces.

Engine Updates

Several subtle changes were made to the exterior of the 1939 engine. Primer cups were no longer offered as an option, so the primer-cup bosses on the cylinder heads were no longer drilled and tapped for the cups (these were the only small-port cylinder heads not drilled for the cups). Parker-Kalon self-tapping screws and unthreaded lower screw plates were used to fasten the rocker covers' top caps. Neoprene-covered spark plug wires were introduced.

A plate with date markings was added just forward of the casting number on the left crankcase. Intake manifold and plumber nut finish was changed to cadmium plate (instead of nickel plate). A drain screw was added

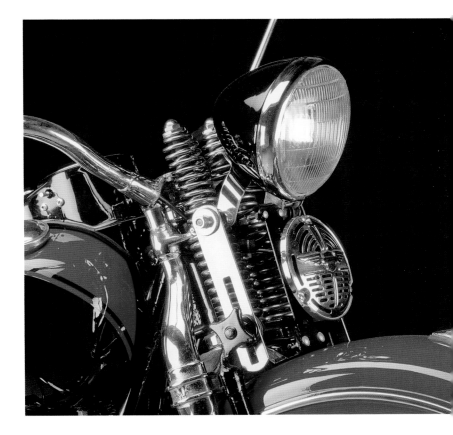

to the carburetor's float bowl, and, because this was the last year the Linkert M-5 was fitted to the Knucklehead, it is a one-year-only carburetor. And the adapter base for the oil-pressure switch was revised, which resulted in a reversion to the 1936–1938-style oil pump body. Late in the production run, the rocker housing was revised to incorporate a casting date plate and thicken the casting in the area around the intake pushrod hole.

Internally, a redesigned pinion shaft was fitted. The 1936–1938 pinion was a two-piece shaft with the helically cut drive gear for the oil pump machined into the outer shaft stub and the pinion gear press-fit on the shaft. Over time, the joint between the two stub shafts would incrementally wear, allowing flex in the shaft; this resulted in a slight misalignment of the gears.

For 1939, the new shaft was machined from a solid bar with six splines running along the axis of the shaft, with the oil-pump gear comprising a separate piece. The pinion-shaft assembly consisted of a one-piece pinion shaft, an oil pump gear spacer, an oil pump drive gear, a spring, and a pinion gear. The new pinion gear for the oil pump is larger in diameter ($1^3/_{16}$ inches versus 1 inch) and

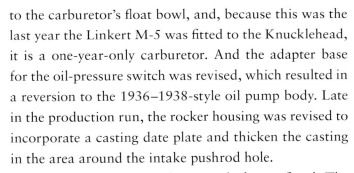

ABOVE LEFT: The fishtail muffler had become a mainstay during the 1930s. This EL has its muffler and muffler tip chrome plated. *Doug Mitchel*

TOP: The springer fork is among the identifiable features of a Knucklehead model. Most springer front ends were painted, unlike this custom chrome-plated fork. *Doug Mitchel*

ABOVE: Helping to underscore the art deco trend, this rear bumper on a 1939 EL help protect the "tombstone" taillight. *Doug Mitchel*

The new bearing for 1939 was much larger and had twenty-five ball bearings, instead of ten. This new bearing was finally strong enough; it was used on H-D Big Twins for more than thirty-five years.

is splined, but it still has five teeth. This one-piece shaft kept the gears in almost perfect alignment. It was used through 1953. The pinion gear was used through 1950.

Mating with the pinion shaft's new, larger-diameter drive gear for the oil pump is a new, smaller-diameter gear ($1^{3}/_{8}$ inches versus $1^{9}/_{16}$ inches), on the oil pump's driveshaft. The result is that the oil pump spins much faster, bringing the system up to operating pressure at lower rpm and generating higher overall oil pressure and flow. Unfortunately, this was a mixed blessing: a quicker rise to operating pressure was certainly advantageous, but the increased flow that came with it resulted in oil-fouled spark plugs and increased oil consumption at low rpm.

To solve the problem, a new relief valve spring was introduced early in the production run; this allows the relief valve to open at 4–6 psi, venting excess oil into the gear case, from which it is returned to the oil tank by the scavenge pump. This went a long way toward reducing the severity of the overoiling problem at low rpm, but it was really just a Band-Aid fix that brought its own penalty, since it also limited available oil pressure at high rpm and wasted much of the pump's output. Harley's engineers must have been satisfied with it, though, because the next attempt to fix the problem would not occur until the 1941 model year.

The old-style straight crankcase breather pipe that had been used since 1936 was replaced by a new pipe with a double elbow that bends forward and then to the left, through a hole in a revised inner primary cover. Inside the primary enclosure, a separate oil deflector attached to the end of the breather tube deflects the oil onto the primary chain. The new inner primary cover is like the previous cover, except that a new hole for the revised crankcase breather pipe was added to the bulge at the rear of the front reinforcing rib, a dimple appeared at the location of the former crankcase breather pipe hole, and the stamped-in boss around the transmission mainshaft hole was made larger.

Rounding out the motor changes for the start of 1939 were pistons that were reinforced with thicker metal behind the third ring grooves and a revised screen on the breather valve. Improved valve springs were also introduced.

A prototype of the 1939 Knucklehead. New features for 1939 that did not make it onto this prototype include the stainless-steel fender side trim strips (note that they are painted in on this bike) and the 1937–1938-style of speedometer light knob. The photo does show the 1939-only Deluxe Solo saddle and saddlebags.

Non-Adjustable Rocker Arm Oiling

Another major change to the engine was made during the production year. Continuing the trend toward simplification and making their machines "idiot proof," H-D finally got rid of adjustable rocker oiling in 1939. With the advent of the fully enclosed rocker covers in 1938, the consequences of overadjustment were no longer as critical because the oil remained inside the covers instead of spraying out to coat bike and rider—yet the risk of squeaking valves and accelerated valve gear wear from underadjustment remained.

The solution was to fit all machines after 39EL1902 with new rocker arms and rocker shafts, with factory-set oiling. The new rocker shafts lack the previous shaft's oil grooves, and the central oil passage ends at two oil holes on the bearing surface, near the right end. The new rocker arms are like the previous arms, except that the oil passage to the valve pad stem ends at a hole on the side of the stem, rather than under the stem. With these new parts, top-end oiling problems were cured at last.

Frame and Forks

The frame used for the 1939 61 OHV was the same as before, except that the steering head was fitted with a self-aligning upper cone to match the self-aligning lower cone that had been introduced in 1938.

The 1939 fork was made easier to service by moving the grease fittings on the spring perch from in between the headlight bosses to the sides of the perch, where they are easily accessible. (The original grease-fitting bosses between the headlight bosses remain, but they are not drilled for the fittings.) To improve the ride, lighter cushion springs were fitted on forks for solo machines; forks for sidecar machines were fitted with the same cushion spring, but an additional cushion spring was fitted in place of the buffer spring. This fork is correct for 1939 through early 1942.

Sliding Gear Transmission

Even though the sliding clutch four-speed, three-speed, and three-speed-with-reverse transmissions introduced on the 1936 Knucklehead had proved to be the only major system free of trouble, H-D introduced a whole new set of Big Twin transmissions for 1939 that incorporated old-style sliding gears for second gear on the four-speed and for first gear on the three-speeds—a seemingly retrograde step. The September 1938 issue of *The Enthusiast* claimed that the change "will make for easier, smoother shifting." In fact, the opposite was true.

What was the real reason for the change? Second gear in the four-speed and first gear in the three-speeds was the gear used most by police and commercial users, and the gears didn't stand up to constant use as well as they should have. These users were in the minority, however, and the more sport-minded riders who were in the majority didn't care for the delay in shifting caused by the sliding gear. In a compromise H-D hoped would satisfy both groups, the sliding-gear second was used only for 1939, while the pair of three-speeds kept the sliding gear first through the end of Knucklehead production in 1947.

The new transmissions had a revised shift pattern, so the shift gates were revised. On the sliding gear four-speed, the neutral position was between second and third (rather than between first and second), so the markings on its shift gate were changed accordingly. Depth of the gate's high-gear notch (fourth on four-speeds, third on three-speeds) was reduced by a half to ease shifting out of high. The gate for the four-speed transmission gate was a 1939-only part. The gate for the three-speeds was used through 1946.

The final changes to the 1939 transmissions were a new starter clutch designed to work with the new 25-ball throwout bearing, shifter fingers revised to include rollers, and a midyear shifter cover revision to include a cast-in date mark on the inside. These changes were carried forward to the next year's transmissions.

Brown Saddles

The 1939 standard solo saddle was like the previous saddle, except that the leather was rhino-russet-grain horsehide instead of black cowhide. Harley-Davidson literature described it as "a beautiful two-tone russet, and it is embossed with a classy appearing rhino grain. In use, the saddle will gradually turn a deep, rich brown as it absorbs the ultra-violet rays of the sun." This seat is correct for 1939 only.

The 1939 deluxe solo seat was also covered in brown horsehide, but it featured a three-piece leather skirt. The rear part of the skirt is shorter than the longer side-skirt lobes, for clearance between the skirt and the fender. The two side skirts are sewn to the center skirts. At the center of the rear skirt is a trim piece that has a floral design under a clear piece of convex glass. Near the lobed tip of each side skirt is a leather, two-layer rosette with a short leather tassel, matching those on the optional saddlebags. This seat is also correct for 1939 only.

Police Models

Radio-equipped police bikes were given revised shielding that permits the use of a standard ignition cable. The new shielding includes a Bakelite insulator where cable connects to spark plug. Radio speakers on all bikes built from October 1, 1938, and after were of the dynamic rather than the magnetic type.

The aluminum projector shell on the Sterling-Harley-Davidson rear-wheel police siren was held in position with six screws with shakeproof washers.

FOR *Thrills* OF A LIFETIME

A NEW 1939 HARLEY-DAVIDSON

More Powerful, Easier Riding, Smarter Looking Than Ever!

HERE'S first news of the great 1939 Harley-Davidson motorcycles—packing great thrills for the red-blooded, sports-loving, outdoor enthusiast. Improved motor performance — still lower upkeep—super-streamlined design—classy appearance — striking new color combinations — and many other outstanding features and refinements. A "mount" that opens up a whole new world of fun and excitement in that greatest of outdoor sports — motorcycling. Be one of the first to ride a new 1939 Harley-Davidson — have lots of good times — see the sights — make new friends — go on jaunts with other happy riders. Go in for gypsy tours — hillclimbs — reliability runs and other thrilling events that provide more real pleasure than you ever dreamed possible.

See the new 1939 models at the Harley-Davidson dealer. Swing into the saddle for a free ride — ask about his Easy Pay Plans—and send in the coupon NOW!

HARLEY-DAVIDSON MOTOR COMPANY
Dept. PS-1138, Milwaukee, Wisconsin

Harley-Davidson
WORLD'S CHAMPION MOTORCYCLE

SEND COUPON NOW
FOR CATALOG OF NEW 1939 MODELS

HARLEY-DAVIDSON MOTOR COMPANY
Dept. PS-1138. Milwaukee, Wis.
Send illustrated literature and FREE copy of The Enthusiast, motorcycling magazine. Stamps enclosed to cover cost of mailing.

Name_____

Address_____

111

This Knucklehead was made extra fancy with disc wheels and whitewall tires, which weren't offered on new machines for 1939.

By the end of the 1930s, the deco era was over, and the Knucklehead was in need of a facelift—which it would get for 1940.

Sidecar

Sidecars were given three refinements for 1939. A revised wheel carrier was introduced that can carry a spare wheel fitted with the optional chrome wheel rings. The car's linoleum floor was replaced by a more weather-resistant rubber floor mat for "better footing and a neater appearance." And the sidecar brake crossover-shaft levers were stamped steel for reduced weight.

1939 Production

Overall sales of H-D motorcycles made a slight gain in 1939 of 1.6 percent—nothing to rejoice about, but far more satisfactory than the 30 percent decline in sales in 1938. Once again, the 61 was the star of the lineup, and it was also the only bulwark preventing another sales catastrophe. Sales of the Knucklehead increased by

almost 20 percent to 2,909. Of this total, 2,695 were ELs and 214 were ESs.

Since its shaky debut, the 61 OHV had been refined to become the great American motorcycle of its era. Among American production motorcycles, it offered unmatched speed, sophistication, and power, and it even stood up well against limited-production specialty machines such as the Broughs, Vincent-HRDs, and Crockers. No longer was the Knucklehead as delicate, leaky, or trouble-prone as its peers—even those with the much simpler and less powerful flathead motor. As a result, its sales grew steadily between 1936 and 1939, while sales of its less sophisticated (read, flathead) stablemates and competitors declined. By the end of the 1939 model year, the sexy 61 had clearly proved the Harleys and the Davidsons right in their belief that OHVs were the future. And a bright future it would be!

3

HARLEY-DAVIDSON GOES TO WAR

Want to jump-start an economy? Start a war, or at least begin preparations for one. By summer 1939, President Roosevelt foresaw the conflict and started the process of putting the United States on a war footing. On September 1, 1939, as H-D began assembling its 1940 models, Hitler took the final step toward world war when his troops invaded Poland.

Popular Milwaukee H-D dealer, Bill Knuth (seventh from left) outside the Milwaukee Motorcycle Club's headquarters before departing for a road run to the Shawano rally in 1939. *Herbert Wagner Collection*

OPPOSITE: It wasn't until 1941 that the overhead-valve Big Twin received a boost in displacement to 74 cubic inches. That became known as the FL model. This 1941 is an EL, but both models look the same. *Doug Mitchel*

Later that fall, the US economy came alive as defense spending rose and factories struggled to meet the demand for war material for the US and Allied forces. Ever eager to do its part, H-D was already hard at work designing the WLA and other military motorcycles that kept it busy during the war years.

The United States was not yet in the war, however, so H-D did not neglect its civilian lineup. For 1940, the company introduced the first extensive revamp of its crown jewel, the 61 OHV, a design that had stabilized for model year 1937.

THE WORLD AT WAR, 1940

Acknowledging that the coming conflict would require a steady, experienced hand at the helm, President Roosevelt ran for an unprecedented third term. In November, he won in an electoral landslide.

In Britain, Winston Churchill replaced Neville Chamberlain as Prime Minister and became the symbol of British resolve to fight and win.

On the continent, the Nazi blitzkrieg rolled forth, overrunning Denmark, Norway, Holland, Belgium, Luxembourg, and France. Soon after, the Battle of Britain began as German planes attacked London daily.

Relations between the United States and Japan continued to deteriorate as the year wore on. The crisis on this front reached a high point in July, when FDR banned export to Japan of scrap metal and oil.

The nation was not yet agreed that war was inevitable—or desired. In September, the isolationist America First Committee held a rally in Chicago to blast FDR as a warmonger. More than 60,000 joined in the protest.

Ignoring the arguments of the isolationists, the president vowed to turn America into the "Arsenal of

Harley-Davidson substantially restyled the Knucklehead for 1940.

Art deco was passé in late 1939 when the 1940 models were released, so Harley replaced the art deco transfers with metal tank badges.

Democracy." Early in the year, he had asked for and received the funds to build 50,000 warplanes, followed in July by an allocation of $4 billion for new Navy ships. In November, he convinced Congress to provide half the country's military production to England.

Realizing late in the year that it takes soldiers—not just planes, and tanks, and ships—to win a war, Congress passed the Selective Service Act, instituting the first peacetime draft for the United States.

And, in a somewhat bizarre turn of events, Harley-Davidson was asked to bid on building copies for the US Army of the German BMW motorcycle that had given Hitler's armies their great mobility in their blitzkrieg strategy.

Fred Ham, the California bike cop who set the 24-hour record in 1937 on a Knucklehead, was killed on December 9 when a car crossed in front of his bike during a high-speed chase.

THE 1940 KNUCKLEHEAD

The OHV Big Twin model line for 1940 included only the high-compression 40EL Special Sport Solo and the medium-compression 40ES twin with sidecar gearing. A special police package was offered for the second year in a row, but for 1940 this only included the three-speed transmission and medium gearing, not the medium-compression motor. All models were listed at a retail price of $430 ($5 less than in 1939) and had to be ordered with one of the option groups, at additional cost. A four-speed transmission was standard, but a three-speed transmission could be specified at the time of order for no additional cost. For $5 extra, the three-speed-with-reverse transmission could be ordered. Speedster handlebars could be substituted for the standard bars for no extra cost.

For 1940, the option groups were reshuffled and a new one was added. The Standard Solo Group was no longer offered, its place as the most basic trim package taken by the new Utility Solo Group. Included in this package were only the most rudimentary "options," such as front safety guard, steering damper, jiffy stand,

and four-ply tires; the last should have been included in the base price, but they were added for $11 extra. Would anyone really want a new motorcycle without tires or a sidestand? The basic package for sidecar and package truck machines was renamed the Utility Group, which included the front safety guard, steering damper, and four-ply tires for $8.50.

The midlevel option package, also new, was the Sport Solo Group, which included a front safety guard, steering damper, jiffy stand, air cleaner, trip odometer, fender light, chrome rims, chrome exhaust pipe covers, colored shift ball, and four-ply tires—all for $22.50.

For a really "doggy" machine, the Deluxe Solo Group was offered. This group ($46) included a front safety guard, steering damper, jiffy stand, air cleaner, ride control, trip odometer, fender light, deluxe saddlebags, deluxe solo saddle, colored shift ball, four-ply tires, and Chrome Group (chrome-plated rims, handlebars, headlight, instrument panel, relay cover, exhaust pipe covers, license frame, and top fender strips).

Styling Changes

With model year 1940 came the first major restyle of the Knucklehead. Unlike earlier restyles, this one was more than paint deep. The machine's look was modernized through use of revised gas tanks, new tank emblems, all-new footboards, and a reshaped toolbox. Overall, the restyle could be called "speed-lined and streamlined." Like the styling cues set on the first series of Knuckleheads, those set in 1940 would be resurrected by the company in later years, most recently and conspicuously on the 1997 Springer Heritage Softtail.

Tanks and Fenders

The most obvious styling changes were the new paint scheme and tank emblems. Gone with the 1930s were the art deco tank transfers that had fit the mood of the prior decade so well, replaced by teardrop-shaped emblems in chrome-plated stamped brass. The company name is debossed down the centerline of the emblems, and the name is framed above and below by a pair of tapered "speed-lines." Speed-lines are painted black, with letters painted red. This emblem is correct for 1940–1946.

This bike has most of the features of the Chrome Group for 1940, which was part of the Deluxe Solo Group and included chrome-plated rims, handlebar, headlamp, instrument panel, relay cover, exhaust pipe covers, license frame, and top fender decoration.

This 1940 EL has the classic post seat that moves up and down on a pogolike hydraulic damper system. That and the 16-inch balloon tires helped smooth the ride for the rigid-frame bike. *Doug Mitchel*

This bike is reported to be an original-paint machine, which means it must have been special-ordered in this color. Standard colors for 1940 were Clipper Blue with white stripe, Flight Red with black stripe, Squadron Gray with Bittersweet stripe, Black with Flight Red stripe, and Police Silver with black stripe.

Each gas tank was fitted with a single, horizontal mount for the tank emblem.

Also gone are the tank panels that had made the 1939 61 so distinctive. Instead, tanks were painted one solid color, except for a pinstripe that starts just forward of the tank badge and sweeps up and back toward the aft end of the tank before jogging forward horizontally, ending several inches aft of the tank emblem. Overall, the pinstripe suggests a projected shadow that frames the emblem perfectly.

Standard colors were black with Flight Red stripe, Clipper Blue with white stripe, Squadron Gray with Bittersweet stripe, Flight Red with Black stripe, and Police Silver with black stripe (police only). Fenders were

painted the same color as the tanks and fitted with the same classy stainless-steel trim stripes as in 1939.

In addition to the tank emblem, the left tank features the "instant-reserve" fuel valve, an innovative feature that controls the flow of fuel from both tanks through one valve, replacing the separate petcocks that had been standard since 1936. This new valve makes it much easier for the rider to turn the fuel on and off—and especially to access the reserve fuel supply without burning his or her hands on the cylinder head. The valve mechanism is fully enclosed within the tank, with only the knob visible on the top of the tank, just to the left of the speedometer. Unscrew the knob to the top of the threads to access the main gas supply. Lift the

Since the 1910s, mechanics from around the world have been trained to properly service and repair Harley-Davidson motorcycles at the Milwaukee plant. Seen here is the Service School graduating class of 1937. Long-time Service Department manager Joe Ryan kneels at far right. *Herbert Wagner Collection*

knob up and away from the tank to access the reserve. A spring-loaded neoprene backing holds it in the reserve position. Reserve capacity is ¾ gallon.

Left and right fuel tanks are interconnected by a coiled balance line that attaches to a nipple fitting on the front underside of the right tank and the fuel valve on the right tank. They act as one tank when the bike is upright and draining. Unfortunately, they still act as one when the bike is on its sidestand and is being filled. If the right tank is filled first, the gas will flow through the balance tube and fill the left tank, too—and this tendency sometimes results in a bit of Harley hilarity.

At their first fill, neophyte Knucklehead riders often get a lesson they'll never forget when, after completely filling the right tank, they then pull off the left tank's gas cap. Their eyes bug out as fuel unexpectedly gushes out and over the hot engine of their new mount. It's pretty comical watching them trying to decide whether to run for their lives from what they imagine will be an imminent explosion, or run for the nearest paper towel to wipe the gas off the bike's paint.

Like the balance line, the fuel line is an all-new part. It runs unbranched from a tapered-flare-nut fitting at the tank's fuel valve to a tapered-flare-nut fitting at the bottom of the fuel filter. This gas line was used only for 1940 and 1941; in 1942, a revised line was fitted for a side-feed gas filter.

ABOVE LEFT: This machine also carries the "airplane-style" speedometer that is correct for 1941–1946 Knuckleheads. The correct tripmeter-equipped speedometer for 1940 is the "white-face" 120-mph speedometer with 2-mph hash marks that was introduced in 1938.

ABOVE: The fender top trim for 1940 included a chevron and stripes for the front fender. The chevron is visible just ahead of the fender light.

LEFT: Oddly, this unrestored 1940 machine is fitted with the 1939-only shifter gate.

ABOVE: In addition to all the correct chrome bits included in the Chrome Group, this bike has many extra chrome-plated parts, including the primary cover and the rear chain guard.

BELOW: Starting in 1941, the redoubtable 61 was joined by a larger OHV stablemate, the 74-ci Models F and FL, created by boring and stroking the 61. This excellent 41 EL was restored by Elmer Ehnes.

What looks like a scene out of the 1954 film, *The Wild One*, actually took place outside of Milwaukee seventeen years before that Hollywood production was made. Milwaukee Motorcycle Club members negotiate a turn on a dirt road. *Herbert Wagner Collection*

Ribbed Gear-Case Cover

After four years of plain, flat, featureless gear case covers, the gear-case cover was revised for 1940 to harmonize with the flowing lines of the rest of the motorcycle. The new sand-cast gear cover is internally the same as the previous cover (with cast-in baffle plate and breather tunnel), but the outside of the casting was given eight ¼-inch-wide horizontal "cooling" fins. "Strength is added and heat is dissipated," according to the September 1939 issue of *The Enthusiast*.

Most 1940 machines were fitted with these sand-cast covers, but the cover was revised again very late in the production season, and the very last 1940 machines were fitted with a completely redesigned cover. This cover is die-cast, resulting in a smoother appearance. Externally,

bulges for the breather tube passage and pinion bushing boss project beyond the base surface of the cover, but not beyond the level of the ribs. Internally, a riveted-on baffle plate (three rivets are used) replaces the cast-in baffle plate used on the previous cover, and the word "ALCO" and the number "97-403" are cast in relief. This cover is correct for very late 1940 through 1947.

Fat Tires

It doesn't matter whether they're on a Deuce Coupe hot rod, a lifted four-by-four truck, or a 1940 Harley —fat tires can give the meekest machine the aura of performance. Usually, the aura is all you really get. The bike we're talking about here, the 1940 Knucklehead, was one of the early pioneers of this trend, but it was

ABOVE: The most obvious changes for 1941 was the addition of stainless trim strips fore and aft of the tank badge.

RIGHT: Also new for 1941 were the "rocket fin" muffler and exhaust Y-pipe (the pair replacing the fishtail muffler with integral pipe).

an accidental trendsetter. And, actually, H-D was following the lead of aftermarket companies like Wolfe and Goulding. G. R. Wolfe was first, designing a special disc wheel and talking General into building a special 5.5x16-inch tire called the Dual 10, with "squeegee action" tread. This was offered for sale in the April 1938 issue of *The Motorcyclist*. The Wolfe Safety Wheels were custom-built on the customer's hubs and a set of wheels, tires, tubes, and flaps sold for $59.00. They were heavy, though—shipping weight was listed as ninety-four pounds! These wheels are shown on Eldon Brown's 1939 61 in this chapter.

For 1940, fat 16-inch tires were made optional on all H-D models. While style was almost certainly considered, the fatter tires were fitted for a more functional reason: they could be run at lower pressure so that the

More subtle changes included a steering-head angle increased to twenty-nine degrees to help stabilize the 16-inch tires.

A new oil pump with centrifugally controlled bypass was another change to the engine for 1941.

sidewalls could flex more than those on the 18-inch tires, absorbing the effects of small road bumps and compensating somewhat for the lack of damping on the front fork and the complete lack of suspension in the rear.

Problem was, the frame's twenty-eight-degree steering-head angle had been set up for the standard 18-inch tires, so machines fitted with the 16-inch tires didn't handle properly. At low speeds, the steering was heavy,

while at high speed the front end gave poor feel and could easily go into a scary wobble on bumpy roads. Savvy riders cured this problem by having their frame "bumped"—bent using a frame jig and press, or by simply hitting the frame's backbone just behind the steering-head with a heavy mallet—to increase the steering head angle slightly. H-D even recommended that their dealers resort to such measures to fix bikes with chronic

handling problems, but I doubt the dealers really told their customers the disturbing details of the fix.

Despite the handling problems, most riders opted for the bigger tires, probably because they liked the look. But opinion was mixed on the looks at the time, as it remains today. More traditional riders felt that the fat tires disrupted the OHV's sleek lines and were the ruin of a fine-handling machine. The factory liked what their customers liked, so fashion won out, and the 16-inch tires became standard the following year.

As mentioned above, the fat tires started a trend, and that trend came to be the great equalizer among American motorcycles: Indian began fitting their machines with the fat tires in 1941, transforming their looks—and ruining their handling forever, too.

A Few More Horses

Styling, schmyling, I say. The real changes for 1940 were all inside the motor. This was a bike for the new decade, after all, and H-D intended to start the new era right. "Harley-Davidson engineers corralled a few more horses and packed them into the new 61 OHV motor," bragged the September 1939 issue of *The Enthusiast*. And all they had to do to get those extra horses was open the gate a bit wider by enlarging the intake ports, intake manifold, and carburetor.

Large-Port Cylinder Heads

New head castings were introduced for 1940 with larger intake ports and a larger-diameter threaded hole for the new, larger intake nipple on the new, larger manifold. Missing from the new casting was the boss for the primer cups, since the cups were no longer offered. Except for these changes, the head castings were like the 1939 castings: they have the latest reinforcements to the rocker brackets (introduced in late 1938), the stamped-in casting numbers 119-35 for the front head and 119-352 for the rear head on the undersurface of the bottom cooling fin on the left side of the head, and the casting date plate near the casting number. These head castings are correct for 1940–1947 civilian Knuckleheads (the few military OHVs built had a unique set of head castings with small ports on large-port castings).

Carburetor and Intake Manifold

The real key to opening the corral gate was the Linkert M-25 carburetor fitted to the 1940 Knucklehead. The M-25 is a 1½-inch carburetor with a $1^5/_{16}$-inch venturi, replacing the venerable Linkert M-5 1¼-inch carb with a $1^1/_{16}$-inch venturi. Four bolts (instead of three) mount the new carburetor to a flange on the manifold. With its ¼-inch-larger venturi, the M-25 added noticeably to the Knucklehead's top end, but at a cost in low-end power and throttle response, so it was used on the 61 only for 1940 (although it was also used on the early 1941 74-ci OHVs). In a cost-cutting move, the new carburetor was painted silver instead of being nickel plated.

Better performance was the goal, so the intake manifold was completely redesigned to carry the increased flow from the larger carburetor. Previous manifolds had been Y-shaped, but the 1940 manifold was reshaped to T section, with $1^9/_{16}$-inch-diameter brass tubes (rather than $1^3/_8$-inch cast iron) in each section. The manifold's carburetor flange is drilled for four mounting bolts, and the cylinder head ends have a smooth bushing surface. New, larger-diameter plumber nuts and brass bushings slide onto the bushing surfaces to fasten the manifold to the new, larger-diameter intake nipples. Manifold and plumber nuts were cadmium-plated.

While the new, larger intake provided the gateway for more fuel-air mixture to flow from the carburetor to the intake ports, a flaw in its design also allowed air to leak in, resulting in backfires, misses, and poor performance. The problem was that the bushings and manifold were both made of brass. Time and vibration would make the bushing gall and seize on the manifold, ruining the seal. Because of this problem, the brass manifold was used for 1940 only; it would be cast iron starting in 1941.

Other Top-End Changes

To handle the increased horsepower produced by the new carburetor and intake tract, the cylinder castings were revised so that the tunnels for the head bolts extended through five cylinder fins instead of four. Except for this one change, the cylinders are unchanged. New head bolts, $5/_{16}$ inch longer than the superseded bolts, pass through the tunnels to fasten the heads to the cylinders.

These cylinders and bolts were fitted for 1940–1947.

With the advent of fully enclosed rocker covers in 1938, problems of oil leaking out had been solved. But there was still the matter of over- or underoiling of the intake valves. Too much, and the bike would suck oil in past the intake valve stem to smoke and foul the spark plugs; too little, and the valves would squeak and wear.

The underoiling problem was solved when fixed oiling for the valve gear was introduced in mid-1939, but some individual engines were still prone to sucking in oil when used hard. This problem was finally solved on the 1940 engine with revised guides for the intake valves. The new guides have a taper at the top that deflects oil spray away from the valve stem and also causes accumulated oil to flow away from the stem. The new guide was used only in the intake position and for 1940–1947.

To seal another source of oil seepage, the lower push-rod covers were redesigned for 1940 to have a flange at the bottom to rest on top of the lower cork seal (previous covers lacked the flange and were pushed down inside the cork seal). To make removing the pushrod-cover retainer easier, the retainer was revised with a small "handle" through which a small screwdriver blade could be inserted to pry out the retainer. The new lower cover and retainer were chrome plated. These parts are correct for 1940–1947 (except that they were Parkerized for 1943–1946).

Brothers and rival dealers, Ray Tursky (H-D, front) and Erv Tursky (Indian, rear) at Lake Delton, Wisconsin, during a hillclimb in 1938. Bobbed fenders on these competition machines were copied by road riders who wanted their bikes to have the allure and glamour of a racer. *Herbert Wagner Collection*

Among the chassis updates was a redesigned brake hand lever.

Stock clutch-and-chain inspection covers were panted black for 1941; chrome covers were available through the accessory catalogs.

ABOVE: A new clutch was introduced on all the Harley-Davidson Big Twins for 1941, to handle the extra power of the 74 OHV.

LEFT: Starting in 1941, standard taillight covers were painted black.

ABOVE LEFT: For 1941, the speedometer was given a facelift to the "airplane style" shown. This particular speedometer is the one supplied when either the Sport or Deluxe group was ordered, so it features a trip odometer. This speedometer has a trip odometer window, just aft of the pointer pivot, that displays three digits (two for miles in black on a white background, and one for tenth-miles in red on a white background), and the main odometer displays only five digits, all for miles and none for tenth-miles.

ABOVE RIGHT: The reset for the tripmeter was on the right side of the dash.

BELOW: This restoration lacks the patent decal Harley-Davidson affixed to the left side of the tank.

Bikes were so simple and parts so interchangeable in the classic days that "Indian Joe Campbell" of Milwaukee kept a spare 80-inch side-valve engine that he swapped into this 61 OHV machine, 40EL1584. Campbell's nickname, "Indian Joe," came about when he once dared to ride an Indian motorcycle to his job as a frame builder at the Harley-Davidson factory. His pals there never let him forget it. *Herbert Wagner Collection*

Bottom-End Updates

The 61's bottom end was revised extensively for 1940 to strengthen it and to equalize the amount of oil reaching the two cylinder walls. The strength was provided by a beefier crankpin and bearing, and the oiling was improved through revisions to the crankcases, connecting rods, and pistons.

Larger Crankpin and Bearing

To handle the added power supplied by the new top end, a new, larger-diameter crankpin was introduced. The 1940 crankpin was given a 1¼-inch-diameter bearing surface (⅛ inch larger than before). The same

length as the previous crankpin, it retains the oil hole and passage from the end to the bearing surface as well as the taper at each end from 1⅛ inches to 1 inch, but now it "steps down" suddenly from the outboard ends of the bearing surface to the start of the taper. This means that the new crankpin can be used with the old flywheels. The new, matching main bearing is ⅛ inch larger in diameter and has fifty-four rollers (instead of forty-two) for a substantial increase in strength. Both crankpin and bearing remained in use through the end of the Knucklehead line in 1947.

New lapping machinery at the factory was put to good use for 1940 production by line-lapping the pinion and sprocket shaft races to ensure perfect sizing and perfect alignment. To make line-lapping possible, new bearing races were introduced that were missing the steel plate formerly used with each race. After the crankcases were bolted together and line-bored, the new bushings were installed and lapped together. The crankpin and roller bearings were also lapped to "glass smoothness." The result? Smoother, quieter, longer-lasting motors.

Crankcase Oil Control

Because the flywheels spin clockwise when viewed from the right side of the engine, much more oil is slung off them onto the walls of the rear cylinder than onto the front cylinder. To block the bulk of this spray, the 1936–1939 motors had a baffle covering the rear half of the rear cylinder opening. The front cylinder opening had a full baffle to increase vacuum below the piston, with the hope that the vacuum would draw in enough air-oil mist to lubricate the cylinder. This arrangement had worked fairly well—the extra oil on the rear cylinder tending to carry away heat, compensating somewhat for the lack of direct cooling air on the rear cylinder—but H-D decided they could do better, so the company gave a new system a try on the 1939 side-valve Big Twins.

On the 1939 side valves, the baffles at both cylinder openings were removed, the positions of the connecting rods reversed (the female rod was moved to the rear cylinder position and the male rod to the front), and half of the slot around the big end of the female rod closed. Why? The new rod positions tended to sling much less oil on the rear cylinder, so the rear baffle wasn't needed to block direct oil spray. And the half-filled slot on the female rod's big end tended to catch oil and throw it on the front cylinder, so the front baffle plates were no longer needed.

The revised female rod slung enough oil on the front cylinder that H-D found it necessary to fit the front piston with an oil control ring for the first time, so now both front and rear pistons had the same ring configuration: two compression rings and one oil control. Side benefits were more consistent vacuum throughout the lower end and less oil mist, easing the burden of the crankcase breather valve and oil separator. This system worked so well that H-D introduced it to the OHV Big Twins for 1940, and the same basic system is still in use on H-D Big Twins today.

The new system for the Knucklehead required new left and right crankcases and front and rear connecting rods. The 1940 crankcases are similar to the previous case, but the baffle plates and steel plates for the sprocket- and pinion-shaft bearing races were omitted and the casting number and date plate moved to inside the case. The left case bears a new casting number, 112-406, and the right case bears casting number 112-404. These cases (set up for the new rod positions and bearing races, but still designed for 8⅛-inch-diameter flywheels) are correct for 1940 only. The new rods bear casting number 40A 706 (male) and 40A 705 (female) and were good enough that they remained in service through the early 1970s.

The final lower-end update for 1940 was to the pinion-shaft assembly. The spacer that had been in between the left side of the oil pump gear and the bearing was replaced for 1940 by a seal ring. Also, a spacer was added between the right side of the pump gear and the spring that fills the space between the pump gear and the pinion gear. Both these changes were used through the end of Knucklehead production in 1947.

Transmission and Clutch

For 1940, the standard transmission was once again the constant-mesh four-speed, because 1939's four-speed transmission with sliding second gear had not been popular among solo riders. Shifting between the constant-mesh first gear and sliding second required more deliberate effort than between the constant-mesh first and second of the pre- and post-1939 four-speeds. Perhaps worse than the slower shifting, neutral was in an odd position on the 1939 transmission—between second and third—making it necessary to shift through second when shifting from first to neutral or from neutral to first.

Although it meant swallowing a bit of pride and a lot of design effort, switching back to the constant-mesh four-speed was the right thing to do. It was the standard transmission through the end of Knucklehead production in 1947. Returning with the four-speed was the 1-N-2-3-4 (front to rear) shifter gate. This gate is correct through 1946.

The sliding-gear transmissions were more popular with police and commercial users, however, so the three-speed and three-speed-with-reverse transmissions with sliding-gear first were optional again for 1940-and-later Knuckleheads.

All the 1940 transmissions were updated with the breather on the transmission case (rather than on the starter cover) for 1940. This change required a new transmission case with a boss for the transmission vent plug, and a new starter cover with an undrilled vent boss. The case and cover were otherwise unchanged.

To reduce chatter and take up slack to prevent rattle, four-slotted spring keys were added to each lined clutch disc. These spring keys fit into the keyways of the clutch ring.

Frame

Only one significant change was made to the frame for 1940: a horizontal toolbox bracket is riveted to the frame's toolbox strap. Starting in 1941, the bracket became a separate piece.

Front Brakes

Front brakes were further refined for 1940. The flimsy, stamped front brake drum was at last replaced by a cast nickel-iron drum with an integral stiffening ring to reduce the vibration and chatter caused by flexing of the drum. The stiffer drum allows use of a new brake-shoe operating shaft that is $9/32$ inch narrower. It also made possible smoother, more uniform grinding of the braking surface for even smoother braking action. Although the front brake was still next to worthless, the 1940 changes made it as good as it would ever get. This drum was used on all spring-fork civilian Big Twins from 1940 through 1949. Interestingly, the Empire Electric Brake Co. began marketing the Magdraulic Electric Brake for H-Ds, promising increased stopping power with "The light touch of a Woman's Hand!"—all for $22, according to an ad in *The Motorcyclist* of April 1940.

Front brake shackles and studs received minor updates to make maintenance easier. The fork-end grease fitting was omitted on the shackle because it was difficult to access. Replacing the shackle grease fitting was a grease fitting on the new nut that secured the shackle to the stud. The grease fitting extended to the left from the end of the nut for unrestricted access. Grease pumped through the fitting was channeled through the nut and along a flat ground into the stud's shaft to grease the shackle. The new shackle and stud are correct for 1940–1947.

Police Models

In addition to the improvements made to the regular civilian motorcycles, police models were available with updated radios and antennas for 1940.

1940 Production

As the US economy improved, more people had money to spend on motorcycles. H-D's sales rose 26 percent overall to a total of 10,461, the highest since 1937. Knucklehead sales rose almost 40 percent, to 4,069. Of this total, 3,893 were ELs and 176 were ESs. Most significantly, the 61 OHV—the most expensive bike in the lineup—was also the best selling for the first time ever.

THE WORLD AT WAR, 1941

FDR saw the US entry into the war as inevitable, so the preparations continued at full throttle. In January, he asked for a defense budget of $10.8 billion. In March, Congress passed the Lend-Lease Act, empowering the president to "lend" arms and equipment to the Allies.

In June, US Army troops were sent in to break up a manufacturing strike that had threatened the production of new warplanes. Hitler, flush with confidence over the successes of his armies, launched an ill-fated invasion of Russia.

In September, the *USS Greer* was attacked by a German U-boat, and FDR ordered US forces to attack on sight any Axis vessels in US waters. Taxes were increased sharply to raise money for the defense buildup.

In October, the hawkish Gen. Hideki Tojo took control of the Japanese government. In November, the US ambassador to Japan warned of an imminent attack on the US military, but the warnings went unheeded. In early December, FDR forwarded a personal appeal for

Elmer Ehnes's restorations always show near-perfect attention to correct finish on parts. This one is not an exception.

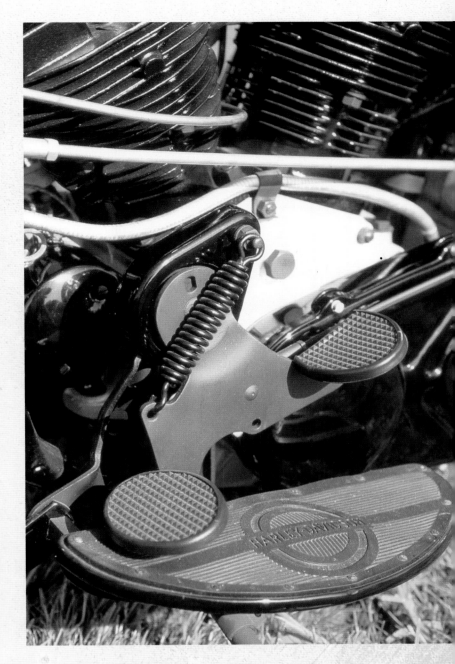

The revised clutch pedal and bracket for 1941.

peace to Emperor Hirohito. Then, on December 7 . . . well, you know what happened: Pearl Harbor. And the end of civilian motorcycle production for the duration.

THE 1941 KNUCKLEHEAD

The OHV Big Twin model line expanded in 1941 to include four models: the high-compression 41EL and 41FL Special Sport Solos, and the medium-compression 41ES and 42FS twins with sidecar gearing. The new

F-series machines were identical to the E-series, except that the F-series were fitted with a 74-ci version of the OHV engine. The EL and ES models were listed at a retail price of $425 ($5 less than in 1940), the FL and FS models at $465. All models had to be ordered with one of the option groups, at additional cost. A four-speed transmission was standard, but a three-speed transmission could be specified at the time of order for no additional cost. For $5 extra, the

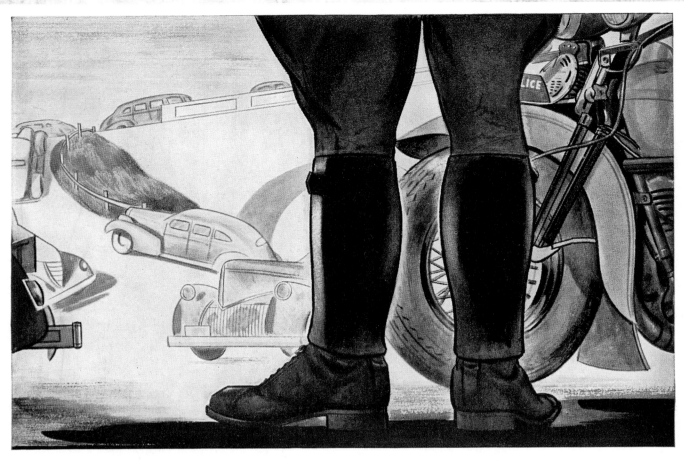

AND HUNDREDS OF CARS...
Slowed Down!

TIME — Any Week End or Holiday
PLACE — Any Important Highway

AN officer and his motorcycle stationed at a dangerous intersection — streams of speeding motor cars—drivers eager to "make time." Like magic, the drivers slow down as soon as the officer and his motorcycle come into view. Traffic proceeds smoothly and safely.

Multiply the number of accidents *prevented* at this spot by the number of similar motorcycle officers on duty — and you realize the unique value of motorcycles in controlling the nation's traffic!

More than 3500 police departments in the United States prefer dependable Harley-Davidson Police Motorcycles — service-proved through the years—for outstanding superiority in performance with an unmatched record of low-cost operation and maintenance.

HARLEY-DAVIDSON MOTOR CO.
Milwaukee   Wisconsin

HARLEY-DAVIDSON
THE POLICE MOTORCYCLE

three-speed-with-reverse transmission could be ordered. The 5.00x16-inch tires that had been optional in 1940 were standard for 1941 (except when the Standard Group for sidecars was ordered); the 4.00x18-inch tires were optional for no extra cost. Speedster handlebars could also be substituted for the standard bars at no extra cost.

For 1941, the Utility Solo Group and Sport Solo Group were unchanged. The Deluxe Solo Group included a front safety guard, steering damper, jiffy stand, air cleaner, ride control, trip odometer, fender light, deluxe saddlebags, chrome saddlebag plates with jewels, deluxe solo saddle, colored shift ball, 5.00x16-inch tires, and Chrome Group (chrome-plated rims, handlebars, headlight, instrument panel, taillight housing, relay cover, exhaust pipe covers, license frame, and top fender ornament).

The 1941 Knuckleheads were available in six standard colors for 1941: Brilliant Black, Skyway Blue, Flight Red, Cruiser Green, or Police Silver (police only).

Styling Changes

Styling for 1941 was largely unchanged from that of 1940, the major exceptions being the addition of trim strips to the gas tanks, a restyled speedometer, and a redesigned muffler. In addition, the taillight cover was painted gloss black (rather than the color of the tanks and fenders).

"Airplane-Style" Speedometer

After five years with the "white-face" style of speedometer, a restyled speedometer was released for 1941 that was influenced by the modern instrumentation in the prominent high-performance aircraft of the day. This new face is difficult to describe, so if this explanation doesn't evoke an image, see the photos of it in this chapter.

Overall, the face has two tones, black and silver, in a bull's-eye pattern. The black center circle is surrounded by a silver circle, which is surrounded by another black circle. The numerals (10 through 120) are silver on the background of the outer black circle.

The hash marks are all short in length and bordered by thin silver pinstripes (one at each end of the hash

Very little changed for 1942, because preparations for wartime production took up most of the company's design engineers' available time. One of the few things that did change for 1942 was a slight redesign of the taillight. To make it easier to assemble the taillight, the internal clips that held the lenses in place were replaced by spring clips fastened by the four straight-slot, cad-plated, countersunk screws down the longitudinal centerline of the taillight cover, as shown here. The side screws shown are not correct; they should be straight-slotted and Parkerized.

marks) that run all the way around the face. The hash marks are spaced at 2-mph intervals, but the marks next to the large numerals are thicker than the intermediate marks. The pointer is thicker than the pointer on previous speedometers and is triangular in section; it is painted white. The odometer window is forward of the pointer pivot and displays five digits, all for miles, in black letters on white background wheels. The tripmeter window is aft of the pivot and displays three digits—two for

On December 7, 1941, just as production should have been hitting full stride in a normal year, the Japanese attacked Pearl Harbor. Virtually all civilian motorcycle production was stopped by the end of the year. For the next 3½ years, the company spent most of its time on military projects, including the manufacture of military motorcycles for the Allies, such as the WLA for the US Army.

miles (in black-on-white background wheels) and one for tenths of a mile (in red on a white background wheel). The speedometer's glass is convex to allow clearance for the thicker pointer, and the bezel is chrome plated. The H-D bar and shield is printed in silver at the aft end of the speedometer face. As the September 1940 issue of *The Enthusiast* boasted, "Even the sleek ships that dart through the skies don't have any smarter-looking dials than this one." This speedometer is correct for 1941–1946.

"Rocket-Fin" Muffler

Like the white-face speedometer, the fishtail muffler had been carried over essentially unchanged from 1936 through 1940, and both had definitely begun to look dated on the restyled 1940 machines. For 1941, the Knucklehead's muffler was completely redesigned for a more modern, "Buck Rogers" appearance, with a stylish rocket fin replacing the fishtail of the old-style muffler.

The new muffler is 3¼ inches in diameter, much larger than the previous muffler, and was redesigned internally. This muffler departed from the standard design practice of the day by not using any steel wool or other internal packing to absorb sound. Instead, it used a resonating chamber to attenuate the exhaust note. The new design had two practical benefits: it didn't grow louder over time, because there was no packing to burn up or blow out; and it reduced back pressure for better engine performance. Even without packing, the new muffler was quieter than the old muffler and had a lower, mellower tone. This muffler is correct for 1941–1949 Big Twins. Standard finish was flat black.

The 1941-and-later muffler lacks the exhaust pipe that is attached to the front of the 1936–1940 muffler, so a new, separate exhaust pipe was introduced to connect the front and rear headers to the muffler. Because of its shape, the new pipe is called the Y-pipe. This pipe was used on all 1941–1947 Knuckleheads. Like the rest of the exhaust, the Y-pipe is painted black.

Big-Inch Knuckle: The FL

Being the quintessential American motorcycle company, H-D eventually came around to raising the Knucklehead's displacement to create a new flagship Big

Rubber was also unavailable for niceties such as footboard mats, so they were stamped of steel.

In Class C competition, guys rode their bikes to events and then competed as shown in this dusty TT scene in 1939. Usage was hard and parts frequently broke, providing much-needed income for dealers and factory alike.

Twin, the 74-ci Series F. Except for its motor, the new model was identical to the venerable Series E.

The extra displacement in the new motor was obtained by increasing the bore by $\frac{1}{8}$ inch (from $3\frac{5}{16}$ inches to $3\frac{7}{16}$ inches) and the stroke by $\frac{15}{32}$ inch (from $3\frac{1}{2}$ inches to $3\frac{31}{32}$ inches). To obtain these new dimensions, the 74s used new cylinders, but these cylinders were based on the same casting used for the 61's cylinders. The result of the displacement increase was about five extra horse-power. To handle the extra power, the lower end and clutch were redesigned for greater strength.

The longer stroke of the 74 made it necessary to use larger-diameter flywheels. The flywheels were made $\frac{3}{8}$ inch larger in diameter than the previous flywheel ($8\frac{1}{2}$ inches versus $8\frac{1}{8}$ inches) and four pounds heavier. In the interest of parts commonality, the 61 engine also used larger castings. The left flywheel has the number—150 403—cast in relief, and the right flywheel has casting number—150 40—cast in relief. Flywheels for the 61 retain the same crankpin hole dimensions that were used on the previous flywheels (tapering from $1\frac{1}{8}$ inches to 1 inch) so that the crankpin was not changed. Flywheels for the 74 are the same as the 61 flywheels, except that the 74's crankpin holes are placed further out for the longer stroke and taper from $1\frac{1}{4}$ inches to $1\frac{1}{8}$ inches for the 74's beefier crankpin. These flywheels were used up to the end of the Knucklehead line in 1947.

The larger flywheels for 1941 would have been too tight a fit in the existing crankcases, so revised cases were fitted for 1941. The left crankcase was substantially revised, with the top two reinforcement ribs extending up to the cylinder bases and the flywheel cavity increased in size for the 8½-inch flywheels. Except for the larger cavity for the new flywheels, the right case was unchanged. Both cases were used from 1941 through 1947.

The stronger crankpin for the 74 OHV has a cylindrical bearing surface that tapers at each outboard end without a "step" to a threaded end (like the 1936–1939 61 crankpin), the larger-diameter bearing surface of the 1940–1947 61 crankpin (1.249 inches versus 1.124 inches), and a new taper, from 1¼ inches to 1⅛ inches. It has the same overall length (3.85 inches) as both previous crankpins. This crankpin was used for 1941–1947.

Carburetors and Intake Manifolds

Because the 1⁵⁄₁₆-inch venturi on the Linkert M-25 had proved to be excessively large on the 1940 61, it was replaced on 1941 61s by the Linkert M-35 1½-inch carb with a 1⅛-inch venturi. The new carb cured problems with low-rpm operation, so it was carried over and fitted to all 61s through 1947.

The M-25 was used on the early 74s but was soon replaced by the Linkert M-75, which was also a 1½-inch carb with a 1⁵⁄₁₆-inch venturi. The M-75 carb was used through the end of 1941 production, after which it was replaced for the following years by the same smaller-venturi M-35 used on the 61s.

In hot climates or in heavy-duty, low-speed use, the OHVs were prone to vapor lock and percolation because the gas in the carburetor would reach excessive temperatures. To fix the problem, the manifold's carburetor pipe was lengthened to space the carburetor farther away from the engine's heat. The 61's manifold is 3¹³⁄₃₂ inches wide, and the 74's manifold is 3⅝ inches wide.

Centrifugal-Bypass Oil Pump

Harley introduced a new oil pump in 1941 to fix a long-standing problem on the OHVs: how to properly regulate oil pump output across the rpm range. To explain the root of the problem, we have to look back to model year 1939. On that year's Knuckleheads, a new, larger-diameter drive gear for the oil pump was added to the pinion shaft and a new, smaller-diameter gear was added to the oil pump's driveshaft, effectively "gearing up" the oil pump drive so that the pump would spin almost twice as fast, resulting in higher oil pressure and greater flow. Unfortunately, this also caused overoiling at low rpm. Later that year, a lighter bypass spring was introduced to help control the overoiling by opening the bypass channel at 4–6 psi, bleeding off the excess oil. The lighter spring reduced the severity of the overoiling problem, but it was really just an expedient fix that also limited available oil pressure and flow at high rpm. Hardly desirable.

The solution for 1941 was both elegant and effective— a new bypass valve controlled by a centrifugal governor that gradually increases oil flow to the engine as rpm rises. At low rpm, the valve is open, venting most of the oil pump's output to the gear case. At high rpm, the valve is closed, sending all of the oil flow to the engine. The new valve gave the 1941 OHVs optimum oiling at all rpm. The pump worked so well, it was used through the end of the Knucklehead line in 1947. The pump is painted silver.

Frames

As mentioned above, the 16-inch tires were standard for 1941. To avoid the handling problems associated with use of bigger tires and a twenty-eight-degree neck angle, H-D "bumped" the early 1941 frames at the factory, bending them for a twenty-nine-degree neck angle. Later frames were given a revised steering-head forging designed for the twenty-nine-degree neck angle. Both 1941 frames also came with two other updates: the toolbox bracket was no longer riveted to the frame's toolbox strap, and the battery was grounded on the frame instead of on the oil line.

7-Inch Air Cleaner

Feeding air to the 1941 carburetors is a new, larger air cleaner. The new air cleaner is superficially similar to

Top Sport for Thrills
—Motorcycling

SOMETHING doing every minute when you ride a Harley-Davidson. You get more fun out of life — visit famous beauty spots — explore distant places — go on glorious vacation trips at little cost. Take in exciting club rallies, hill-climbs, race meets and other thrill-packed motorcycle events. Visit your Harley-Davidson dealer today — see the 1941 models with their airplane styling, zooming power, rugged dependability and important mechanical improvements — and ask about his Easy Pay Plans.

MAIL COUPON NOW

HARLEY-DAVIDSON
WORLD'S CHAMPION MOTORCYCLE

200-Mile National Speedway Championship again won by Harley-Davidson. Louis Guanella first — setting new A.M.A. record. First seven places go Harley-Davidson!

HARLEY-DAVIDSON MOTOR CO.,
Dept. P, Milwaukee, Wis.

Send pictures and descriptions of smart 1941 models. Also FREE copy of big 24-page ENTHUSIAST magazine filled with thrilling motorcycle photos and stories. Stamp enclosed for mailing cost.

Name

Address

The 1941 FL featured the new 74-cubic-inch, overhead-valve Knucklehead engine. The displacement increase helped bump power output to forty-eight horsepower at five thousand rpm, a significant improvement over the the 61-cubic-inch E series. *David Blattel*

the previous air cleaner assembly—the cover fastens to the backing plate with four J-slots, has the bar and shield stamped on the flat surface in the center, and has a data plate riveted to the edge—but it is now 7 inches in diameter, instead of 6 inches. The backing plate was revised so that the filter's mesh and support are removable as a unit from the backing plate, which makes changing or cleaning the air filter easier. The backing plate was Parkerized, and the cover was chrome plated. This air cleaner is correct for 1941–1947 (except that the 1943–1946 covers were painted black).

1941 Production

Much of the total H-D production for 1941 was for the military. Yet H-D still had the capacity to produce a record number of OHV Big Twins for the civilian market—5,149 in all. Of this total, 2,280 were ELs, 261 were ESs, 2,452 were FLs, and 156 were FSs. Then, as now, American riders can never resist bigger engines and more power: the 74 OHVs outsold the 61s 2,608 to 2,541—despite this prediction in the September 1940 issue of *The Enthusiast*: ". . . a limited number of 74 OHV Harley-Davidsons will be produced. However, as I have said, the number will be limited and production will not be nearly as extensive as on the other models."

THE WORLD AT WAR, 1942

By the time the 1942 models began rolling off the line in the early fall of 1941, America was perilously close to entering the war. American factories were churning out planes, tanks, guns, and other military equipment to the exclusion of almost everything else. H-D was pulling its weight in this effort.

With fat contracts to build bikes for US and Allied forces—and increasing shortages of steel, copper, iron, and aluminum—H-D only promised each dealer one new bike for the year. Then came December 7. On January 1, 1942, all production of civilian cars, trucks, and motorcycles was halted.

In the early months of the conflict in the Pacific, US troops were forced steadily back all across this theater. Manila fell in January, and American and Philippine forces withdrew to the Bataan Peninsula. They surrendered there in April, and the Bataan Death March began. About 76,000 Allied prisoners were forced to march to prison camps, and any who were too sick to continue were bayoneted or beheaded where they lay. As many as 10,000 died.

In February, FDR ordered internment for all Japanese-Americans on the West Coast of the US. More than 100,000 were moved inland to internment camps in the following months. Despite this obvious mistreatment of their families, 10,000 Americans of Japanese descent volunteered for the "Nisei" unit of the United States Army.

On February 7, H-D president Walter Davidson Sr. died, and William H. Davidson took his uncle's place at the head of the company.

In April, B-25 Mitchell bombers led by Jimmy Doolittle flew off the deck of the carrier *USS Hornet* and bombed Japan. Damage inflicted was slight, but the morale boost in the United States was immense.

In May, US forces finally slowed the Japanese advance when they fought the Japanese to a draw in the Battle of Coral Sea, with each side losing one aircraft carrier. But the Japanese offensive was far from over: Japanese forces landed in the Aleutian Islands of Alaska. Gasoline and sugar rationing began in the United States.

In June, the United States won its first major victory over the Japanese in the Battle of Midway. The US Navy sank four Japanese carriers and lost one of its own. The then-unknown Maj. Gen. Dwight D. Eisenhower was named commander of US forces in Europe. And $42.8 billion was appropriated for the war effort that year—reportedly more than the entire cost of World War I, but about the price of a squadron of stealth bombers today.

In August, United States forces invaded Guadalcanal, seizing the offensive position from the Japanese. In August, the US Army Air Forces began bombing raids on occupied Europe from bases in England as twelve B-17 Flying Fortresses attacked the railroad marshaling yards at Rouen, France.

In October, the Bell XP-59, the first American jet airplane, took off on its first flight.

In November, the Allies invaded North Africa, and pushed deeper, seeking to drive Field Marshal Erwin Rommel's forces off that continent.

After the war ended, Harley-Davidson resumed civilian production as soon as it was allotted materials to build civilian machines.

In December, gasoline rationing took effect nationwide. Fuel-efficient motorcycles once again appealed to the masses. Unfortunately, only used machines were available.

The 1942 Knucklehead

The OHV Big Twin model line for 1942 included the high-compression 42EL and 42FL Special Sport Solos and the medium-compression 42E and 42F twins. The 61s were listed at a retail price of $425, the 74s at $465—both prices the same as the previous year's. All models had to be ordered with one of the option groups, at additional cost. A four-speed transmission was standard, but a three-speed transmission could be specified at the time of order for no additional cost. Sidecar gearing was available for no extra charge. For $5 extra, the three-speed-with-reverse

transmission could be ordered. The 5.00x16-inch tires were standard. Speedster handlebars could be substituted for the standard bars for no extra cost.

Standard colors were Skyway Blue, Cruiser Green, Flight Red, Brilliant Black, or Police Gray.

For 1942, the same option groups were offered again. The Utility Solo Group included only the most rudimentary "options," items such as front safety guard, steering damper, jiffy stand, and 5x16-inch tires, and black rims. The basic package for sidecar and package truck machines was the Utility Group, which included the safety guard, steering damper, jiffy stand, 5.00x16-inch tires, and black rims.

The midlevel option package was the Sport Solo Group, which included a front safety guard, steering

The first postwar bikes built were like the few built during the war—very plain, with almost no chrome- or cad-plated parts and very limited paint selections. Like almost all wartime-through-1946 bikes, this one was updated with many of the normally plated parts when it was restored, rather than with all the Parkerized parts. It is owned by Larry Engesether.

damper, jiffy stand, air cleaner, trip odometer, fender light, chrome rims, chrome exhaust-pipe covers, colored shift ball, and 5.00x16-inch tires.

The top option package was the Deluxe Solo Group. This group included a chrome-plated front safety guard, steering damper, jiffy stand, air cleaner, ride control, trip odometer, fender light, deluxe saddlebags, set of jewels for saddlebags, deluxe solo saddle, colored shift ball, 5.00x16-inch tires, Chrome Group (chrome-plated rims, handlebars, headlamp, instrument panel, taillight housing, relay cover, exhaust-pipe covers, license frame, and top fender ornament), and several new items: chrome fender tips, clutch and brake pedal rubbers, chrome mirror, and chrome parking lamps. This option package made the Knucklehead flashier than ever—but wartime restrictions soon made it impossible to obtain.

Styling Changes

Styling was unchanged for 1942; even the available colors went unmodified. The lucky few customers who were able to get a 1942 Harley had their choice of Brilliant Black, Skyway Blue, Flight Red, Cruiser Green, or Police Silver (police only).

Finish Changes

Shortages of aluminum and cowhide resulted in changes to some parts for 1942. Aluminum was used to manufacture silver paint, and it was strictly rationed even in late summer 1941 when 1942 production began. This meant that the tappet blocks and oil pump were painted white, instead. They remained white until the restrictions were lifted in 1946. And cowhide was needed to make boots for all the men who were being drafted, so the seats for 1942 were covered in horsehide.

Weathering the War, Part I

With numerous contracts to fill for military motorcycles, H-D was set up to prosper in 1942, despite the war. Not so the company's dealers. With no new machines or parts to sell, and with most of their customers off to war, they would have to be clever to survive.

Knowing the plight of its agents, H-D sought to help by including helpful advice in the dealer bulletins. The

Harley-Davidson fitted the prewar tank trim shown through model year 1946.

factory urged small, remote dealers to take war jobs and to invest their startup money in war bonds so they would be ready with enough money to open their shops again when the war ended.

Many dealers took the advice, becoming police motorcycle officers, soldiers, and shipbuilders. The factory urged dealers to secure as much work on police bikes as possible. And H-D helped woo what scarce customers they could by mailing out over 3,000 posters to police chiefs.

Other helpful advice? In the November 16 dealer newsletter, H-D provided an answer to every dealer's most pressing dilemma, namely, "What can I get in the way of an appropriate Christmas gift for my police chief and other good customers?" The answer? An official H-D memo holder, at a cost of only $1.15 each, if five or more were ordered.

In the November 30 newsletter, dealers were advised to send letters or cards to their police customers to "capitalize on gas rationing and get more service work" by emphasizing how regular service work would minimize their bikes' consumption of scarce fuel. This issue also shared the secret for easy installation of the hard plastic hand grips that had replaced rubber grips that year. The secret? Soak them in hot water before installation.

The newsletter put out in mid-December reminded dealers to pester the chiefs yet again, this time to overhaul police motorcycles during the winter months.

To help secure bikes for their showrooms, H-D urged the dealers to "Try and buy Harley-Davidsons from the boys going to war!"

These bulletins also provide a look at how tightly controlled the supplies of strategic materials had become. Because rubber was strictly regulated, seals for the rocker housings became unavailable in April 1942.

By May, H-D was urging all dealers to send in ruined pistons so that the company could reclaim material to make replacement pistons. Dealers had to supply proof that they had sent in ruined pistons before they could qualify for replacement pistons. All the pistons sent in were pooled "for the common good of all Harley-Davidson dealers." H-D made it very clear that no dealers would get replacement pistons without first recycling old pistons, and that the number of pistons a dealer recycled in no way guaranteed that he would get that many in return. In September, batteries and exhaust valves were restricted to an exchange basis, too.

1942 Production

As mentioned above, Pearl Harbor changed everything just as 1942 production was hitting full stride. Despite the shutdown of civilian production by the start of 1942, H-D records show that 1,743 OHV Big Twins were built. Of this total, 620 were ELs, 8 were ELAs (special ELs for the US Army), 45 were ELCs (special ELs for the Royal Canadian Army), 164 were ESs, 799 were FLs, and 107 were FSs. Those who bought these bikes were fortunate indeed, because no new machines were made available to average civilians until late 1945.

THE WORLD AT WAR, 1943

Steadily gaining strength thanks to America's production abilities, the Allies began pushing back the German and Japanese advances that had previously seemed so easy in 1940 and 1941. But the Allied victories were not without cost: by the start of 1943, more than 60,000 Americans had died in combat.

In January, FDR, Churchill, and Gen. Charles DeGaulle met at Casablanca to discuss war strategy. Sensing that they would ultimately triumph, the Allies agreed that they would accept nothing less than unconditional surrender from Germany, Italy, and Japan. They also agreed to start a second front against Germany by invading Sicily. General Eisenhower was given command of the new front. And the US Army Air Force began a concerted bombardment of Germany.

Around the same time, the Japanese pulled off a stealthy withdrawal from Guadalcanal, and the US

Marine Corps finally took control of the island. In a long battle in February, Gen. George S. Patton's forces turned back a German advance at Kasserine Pass, stopping Field Marshal Erwin Rommel's forces. In the process, Patton's forces suffered 6,000 casualties. The Russians, too, had turned the tide, and the German Army began their long retreat from Russia. In the States, nationwide shoe rationing began.

In March, B-25 Mitchell bombers of the US Fifth Air Force avenged Pearl Harbor by sinking eight fully laden troop transports and four destroyers in the Battle of Bismarck Sea.

In May, the 7th Infantry Division retook Attu Island (in Alaska's Aleutian chain) from the Japanese. Before the battle was over, one thousand surviving Japanese soldiers shouted "Banzai!" and charged the Americans. Five hundred died in the attack, while most of the rest committed suicide. Of the roughly 2,500 Japanese who had been on the island, only 28 surrendered.

In June, income tax withholding was instituted to improve government cash flow.

In July, the Allied armies invaded Sicily, and Mussolini resigned.

In September, Allied armies invaded Italy. Five days later, Italy surrendered.

On September 18, company cofounder and Chief Engineer William S. Harley passed away.

In November, FDR, Churchill, and Stalin met in Tehran, Iran, to discuss the upcoming invasion of Europe.

In December, FDR, Churchill, and Stalin met in Tehran, Iran, and Stalin pledged to join the war against Japan as soon as the war in Europe ended. FDR, Churchill, and Chiang Kai-shek then met in Cairo, Egypt, to discuss the war in the Pacific.

By the end of the year, America was truly the "Arsenal of Democracy." Production of B-24 Liberator bombers topped 500 per month at Ford's Willow Run, Michigan, plant alone. American shipyards cranked out 1,949 ships in 1943, among them were 1,238 Liberty ships.

And H-D was doing its part, too. In 1943, the company built more than 27,000 military motorcycles.

THE 1943 KNUCKLEHEAD

On paper, the OHV Big Twin model line for 1943 included the high-compression 43EL and 43FL Special Sport Solos and the medium-compression 43E and 43F twins. That was the idea, but H-D could build bikes only on special order for customers who had first received War Production Board (WPB) approval, which was very difficult to obtain in 1943. Those bikes that were built were likely available with only the items in the Utility Solo Group—front safety guard, steering damper, jiffy stand, 5.00x16 tires, and black rims.

A source listing the standard colors for the year is hard to find, but gray was probably the only option; if there were other colors available, they may have been leftover from 1942 production and used up on the 1943 models. The only reference to colors for 1943 that I could find was in the September 13, 1943, dealer news bulletin, which stated that colors other than standard were offered on police orders for $5 extra.

The only real changes for 1943 appear to be the virtual elimination of chrome plating, cadmium plating, and silver paint. Nearly everything that had been plated on previous models was Parkerized or painted black for the duration of the war and through at least part of 1946, when restrictions on the use of critical war materials were eased. The one notable exception to this rule is that the stainless-steel tank strips seem to show up on the photos of wartime bikes. H-D must have had enough leftover from previous years to carry them through the war. Some bikes may have been fitted with the earlier, chrome- or cad-plated parts, if any of those parts were left in inventory at the time the bikes were assembled.

What would one of these wartime machines look like? The tank emblems, oil pump, and tappet blocks were painted white. Pushrod tubes, timing hole plug, seat post tube, and almost all the screws and bolts were Parkerized. The bezel on the speedometer and around the dash's indicator lights was painted black, as were the ignition-switch cover, speedometer light knob, tank-shifter and its gate, the handlebar spirals, gas caps, headlamp rim, horn face, front brake hand lever, front fender light cover, air-cleaner cover, covers for the horn and headlight switches, steering damper knob, and gas shut-off knob. The stainless-steel fender strips were left off. The floorboards for 1943–1947 were painted black and were fitted with ribbed steel (instead of rubber) mats. The rubber blocks on the kickstart pedal were also omitted.

Just about the only chrome-plated parts left on the machine were the four rocker-shaft "knuckle" nuts. In short, the lucky few who were authorized to buy a new Harley got what most people would consider to be an ugly duckling rather than a graceful swan. Others like the cleaner, simpler look.

Weathering the War, Part II

War continued to be hell for cash-strapped H-D dealers in 1943, but the factory was there for the dealers again, with more helpful hints in the dealer news bulletins.

Although oil was scarce and rationed, H-D motorcycles didn't know it. They leaked just as much as they had during peacetime, so the oil had to be washed off from time to time with a little Gunk. Cans and glass jars were in short supply, so H-D was forced to discontinue selling Gunk in small containers. For those dealers who'd planned ahead and heeded the factory's advice of the previous year to court police business, good news was presented in the July 20 dealer newsletter: "A plan long under consideration has now been approved by the proper WPB officers, and police departments having a vital need for motorcycles will be allotted machines in late August or early September."

Even more good news and advice was offered in the August 16 issue: "War plants eligible for new H-Ds for guard and police duty!" Dealers were encouraged to visit gunpowder plants, air conditioning factories, gun factories, steel mills, and other essential defense manufacturers to encourage them to apply for WPB approval to purchase motorcycles.

Apparently the police orders began rolling in, because the September 13 issue stated that police bikes ordered with nonstandard colors were $5 extra—implying, of course, that colors other than gray or silver really were available.

Asserting that more H-D commercial motorcycles were "very definitely needed to promote the war effort,"

One way to tell a properly restored 1946 Harley-Davidson EL is by the amount of chrome parts it has—or rather, that it doesn't have. With World War II still fresh in people's minds, materials like chromium for trim remained hard to find. *David Blattel*

the November 1 issue urged dealers to court buyers for such machines. The dealers were told to promote the great potential "savings in rubber, gas, and time" these machines would offer to essential war industries for messengers—and to deliver shipments.

The November 15 issue gave the dealers a little pat on the back by trumpeting the results of the court-your-chief campaign: "137 police departments have qualified for new Harley-Davidsons!" Unfortunately, the bulletin gave no indication of how many bikes were allotted to these police departments or what models they were. However, it did include a "purchase proposal for police motorcycles" to show the dealers the proper way to submit a successful request to the WPB. Soon, even the flimsiest excuse would qualify a police department for new machines.

1943 Production

H-D records list only 203 OHVs in their 1943 production of over 29,000 motorcycles. Of the total, 53 were ELs, 103 were Es, 33 were FLs, and 12 were Fs. These machines were available only to the very well connected (for example, a famous actor or a general's son), and those who could demonstrate a compelling need related to the war effort for a new motorcycle.

THE WORLD AT WAR, 1944

In January, the US march across the Pacific islands continued with the successful invasion of the Marshall Islands.

In late February and early March, the US Eight Army Air Force intensified the bombing campaign against Germany, in a campaign that would come to be known as "Big Week."

In April and May, US forces continued pushing the Japanese from their island strongholds, successfully invading Kwajalein, Eniwetok, Hollandia, and Wake.

In June, the Allies struck their most telling blows to date against the Germans. On the June 4, US forces captured Rome. Two days later, Allied forces invaded France with an amphibious landing at Normandy. FDR signed the GI Bill of Rights.

In August, Allied forces captured Brittany, invaded southern France, and liberated Paris.

In September, Allied armies pushed into Germany, truly taking the war to the Fatherland and signaling that the end was near. Unfortunately, the Germans still had a lot of fight left in them.

In October, US forces returned to the Philippines, and the US Navy thrashed the Japanese navy in the Battle of Leyte Gulf.

In November, FDR won his fourth presidential election, with Harry S. Truman as his vice president. The end for Japan's war effort was also approaching, and Hideki Tojo's military government fell.

In December, German forces began a surprise offensive—the Battle of the Bulge—in the Ardennes. The offensive initially forced back the overconfident Allied armies, but was soon routed. By the time the Germans retreated, almost 77,000 Americans had been killed or wounded.

Throughout most of the desperate fighting of 1944, H-D motorcycles were there. During the year, H-D continued to contribute, building 16,887 military motorcycles.

THE 1944 KNUCKLEHEAD

According to the 1944 order blank, the OHV Big Twin model line for 1944 included the high-compression 44EL and 44FL Special Sport Solos for $425 and $465, respectively, and the medium-compression 44E and 44F medium-compression twins, also for $425 and $465, respectively. Nonpolice solo bikes were available with only the items in the Utility Solo Group—front safety guard, steering damper, jiffy stand, 5.00x16 tires, and black rims. The only standard color listed was gray or silver—the factory's option, not the buyer's.

Wartime restrictions once again prevented any significant changes. The only mechanical change was that a small spring was added to each clutch hub's long studs. Harley's stocks of rubber tires had been depleted, so "S-3" synthetic-rubber tires were fitted. And Linkert's supply of silver paint had been used up, so carburetor bodies were painted black and would remain black even after the war.

Weathering the War, Part III

As the Allies began to get the upper hand in 1944, the

The Knucklehead engine, with its massive rocker covers, is considered a classic design among motorcycle enthusiasts everywhere. *Doug Mitchel*

With the conclusion of World War II, Harley-Davidson got back to the business of building bikes for America's citizens. This 1946 EL was among the first to hit the road in postwar America. *Doug Mitchel*

By midway through model year 1946, Harley-Davidson was finally able to start offering a few shiny extras on new machines. In February 1946, the dealer news bulletins announced that aluminized paint was available, so Police Silver was once again an option and, presumably, the oil pumps and lifter blocks could be painted silver, rather than white.

supply situation gradually loosened up at home. Still, dealers had to scramble to secure enough business to support themselves. Again, Harley's news bulletins were there to help.

The March 20 issue announced triumphantly that "You can get OHV models on your essential civilian and police orders!" providing the first proof, besides the notoriously unreliable production figures the company published, that OHV models were really made for civilian use during the war. The article went on to specify that even the top-of-the-line 74 OHV models were available.

The April 17 issue informed dealers that the resins used in paints were now even further restricted, so the factory could no longer guarantee that replacement tanks and fenders would be painted. Primered parts would be substituted, if paint supplies were exhausted.

Although paint was in short supply, plastic for hand grips apparently was not. The May 1 issue announced that dealers could get all the hand grips they needed, and that these grips would not count against their "parts quota."

As the Allies marched from victory to victory, they naturally captured thousands of prisoners. Many of them ended up in prison camps in the United States and Canada. And all those hapless POWs presented the enterprising Harley dealer with still more opportunity for profit. The June 26 issue claimed that "War prisoner camps present added police problem!" and urged all Harley dealers near the camps to contact the security officials in the camps and police in the area to "acquaint them with the procedures to obtain as many H-D police motorcycles as their needs make necessary."

As these "tips" to the dealers show, the WPB's process of allocating machines where they were needed most had become a farce by mid-1944, and would only get worse (or better) as the year continued.

The October 9 issue recommended that dealers sell the 74 flatheads to all customers because orders could be filled faster than if 61 or 74 OHVs were ordered.

The October 23 issue suggested that dealers buy special H-D pigskin wallets as Christmas gifts for police chiefs and other favored customers.

Although not spoken of in the news bulletins, H-D dealers were gifted with a new source of motorcycles

Chromium was still a scarce commodity after World War II, which explains why many of the initial postwar bikes were composed primarily of painted parts. *Doug Mitchel*

to sell in mid-1944. *Shop Dope No. 233* said, "During the past four months, the Government has sold a large number—possibly 3,000 to 5,000—Army surplus, used H-D military-model motorcycles. . . . Included in the motorcycles already sold are 800 to 900 XA shaft-drive models. . . . A portion of both types of these motorcycles have been purchased by Harley-Davidson dealers."

Showing how loose the regulations had become, the November 20 issue featured a photo of a mine mechanic

The simplicity of the rigid frame is a favorite for custom bike builders today. The locking toolbox was an accessory that, like the EL's frame, has found its place in today's custom bike market too. *Doug Mitchel*

for the Sentry Coal Company of Madisonville, Kentucky, who shuttled between the company's mines on his new 1944 OHV. The issue also trumpeted that 380 police departments recently received approval to buy new motorcycles.

1944 Production

Eligibility criteria were eased somewhat during 1944, so civilian OHV production more than doubled to 535. Of this total, 116 were ELs, 180 were Es, 172 were FLs, and 67 were Fs.

THE WORLD AT WAR, 1945

By the start of 1945, a swift end to World War II seemed a foregone conclusion. The American and British armies were building a bridgehead to cross the Rhine, and the Russians were poised to sweep into Germany. In the Pacific, the US Marines were catching their breath before assaulting the last islands on the way to Japan itself.

ABOVE: This restoration was given a nonstandard two-tone paint scheme using the two regularly offered colors available early that year: red and gray. On February 5, 1946, the gray color was replaced by Skyway Blue.

LEFT: By the end of the year, Harley-Davidson was even able to offer many items in its accessory catalog. Harley's February 18, 1946, dealer news bulletin also specified that chrome fender tips, colored shift ball, and deluxe saddlebags were added to the Special Solo Group, which meant that chrome was becoming available for use on frivolous decoration. Based on the fact that chrome was available for fender tips, it is likely that around this time chrome-plated pushrod tubes, tank emblems, air-cleaner covers, shift levers, shifter gates, and horn covers were also available.

In February, US forces captured Manila. One of the epic battles of the war began with the US invasion of Iwo Jima. The Japanese defenders on Iwo had spent the previous three years preparing over 800 pillboxes to protect the defenders during the expected invasion. The 21,000 Japanese soldiers on the island had been supplied with over 22 million rounds of ammunition and were ordered to fight to the death. The battle would not end for another month.

In March, US forces crossed the Rhine River, one of the last obstacles on the road to Berlin. In the Pacific, the US Marines gained control of Iwo Jima after an incredibly costly battle.

On April 1, US forces invaded the heavily fortified island of Okinawa. Although the landing went almost unopposed, the Americans soon ran into the fiercely determined Japanese defenders.

On April 12, less than one month before the fall of Germany, President Roosevelt died of a cerebral hemorrhage as he posed for a portrait in Warm Springs, Georgia. Harry S. Truman was sworn in as president that afternoon.

On May 7, the war ended in Europe, when Germany surrendered unconditionally. The war with Japan continued.

In June, the American forces on Okinawa gained control of the island. It was one of the costliest victories of the war, however, with over 49,000 Americans killed or wounded. Only the Japanese home islands remained unvanquished.

On July 16, the world entered the nuclear age when the first atomic bomb was detonated in New Mexico.

On August 6, a US B-29 Superfortress dropped an atomic bomb on Hiroshima. The next day, Truman promised a "rain of ruin" if the Japanese did not surrender. They did not answer. On August 8, more than two months after the fighting stopped in Europe, Russia declared war on Japan. The next day, an atomic bomb was dropped on Nagasaki. On August 14, Japan surrendered unconditionally.

On September 2, almost six years after the war began, it officially ended when the formal Japanese surrender was signed on the deck of the battleship *USS Missouri*.

President Truman ordered a full return to consumer production. Back in Milwaukee, H-D gladly followed Truman's order and prepared to grab their hard-earned share of postwar prosperity.

THE 1945 KNUCKLEHEAD

The OHV Big Twin model line for 1945 included three versions of each model, the high-compression 45EL and 45FL Special Sport Solos for $463.67 and $465, respectively, the medium-compression 45E and 45F twins at the same prices as the EL and FL, and the 45ES and 45FS twins with sidecar gearing, again at the same prices as the EL and FL. One has to wonder why anyone would order the 61 models when they were only $1.33 cheaper than the 74 OHVs.

Interestingly, an additional $4.08 ($2.04 per tire) surcharge was levied on the 74 OHV models for their synthetic tires, raising the base price to $469.08. The cost of these tires was built into the base price for the 61 models. The only standard color available was gray.

These bikes were available with the Utility Solo Group—front safety guard, steering damper, jiffy stand, 5.00x16-inch tires, and black rims—which cost $14.50 extra or the Utility Group for sidecar or package truck motorcycles (which was the same as the other utility group, minus the jiffy stand) for $12. Beginning in March, this option group also included a tripmeter, because the non-tripmeter speedometers were no longer available, according to the March 12 dealer news bulletin. The $1.50 extra that H-D added for the tripmeter raised the price of the option group to $16.

The 1945 OHVs were also available with a new option group, the Special Solo Group, which included a front safety guard, steering damper, ride control, jiffy stand, air cleaner, rear safety guard, trip odometer, mirror, 5.00x16-inch tires, sheepskin saddle cover, solo windshield, and black rims—all for $44.50. Beginning in September, a shock absorber replaced the ride control in the Special Solo Group and the group price was raised to $55, according to the September 9 dealer news bulletin. The shock was also available for order without the group for $15. It is not clear whether the bikes built around September 9 were 1945 or 1946 models.

Production of military H-Ds had begun to slow, so there was time to make a few more mechanical improvements for 1945 than had been made in previous wartime years. The generator drive gear's outside diameter was increased from 1 inch to 1.022 inches. The new gear was used through 1947. The spring ring groove was omitted from the clutch pushrod used from 1945 through 1947. And an Oilite bushing replaced the plain bushing and grease fitting on the 1945–1947 clutch pedal bracket.

Weathering the War, Part IV: Final Chapter

Victory was at hand, but the dealers were still fighting a war of their own against shortages of bikes and spare parts—and, of course, government red tape. Once again, however, the dealer news bulletins gave hope that the dealers would survive.

The February 12 issue gave the first indication that parts and accessories would again be available when it announced the reintroduction of Speedster handlebars.

The April 9 issue boasted that 450 police departments were approved to receive new machines.

Even though the Nazis had already surrendered, the May 21 issue made it clear that "V-E Day has brought no change in production of current Harley-Davidsons!" Furthermore, the company asserted that there would be "no special priority on motorcycles for veterans," and that dealers should be "tactful" in explaining the situation to former GIs.

As the war wound down to its conclusion, even more new surplus items were offered through the dealers. The June 4 issue announced that Army saddlebags would be available for $12.50 retail per bag.

The July 30 issue informed dealers that buddy seats were once again available for the 61s, which means they were available for all the Big Twins, since they all used the same seat.

The August 27 issue proclaimed that "A new era dawns with war's end" and promised a swift resumption of civilian production.

Only a week after the surrender of Japan was signed, the September 10 issue revealed that "effective

Except for the special wartime steel parts and finishes, the Knuckleheads built during World War II are just like their prewar counterparts.

Chrome and stainless steel were in short supply.

immediately" a shock absorber for the front forks was included with the new Special Solo Group; the shock was also available separately for $15. The price for the Special Solo Group was raised to $55. The November 12 issue announced the return of black rubber grips to replace the hard plastic grips mandated by the WPB.

Option groups! Accessories! Rubber grips! Normalcy! Thank the Lord! Thank the bomb! And FDR, God rest his soul. The hard times really were over!

1945 Production

As a result of eligibility requirements being further relaxed so that just about any police department could qualify, and the end of the war, H-D's civilian production tripled to 1,430. Of this total, 398 were ELs, 282 were ESs, 619 were FLs, and 131 were FSs.

IT'S BACK TO A KNUCKLEHEAD WORLD, 1946

With the war over, life at home slowly returned to normal. FDR's New Deal was replaced by Truman's Fair Deal, as in "every segment of our population, and every individual, has a right to expect from his government a Fair Deal."

But after four years of restrictions on their right to strike and frozen wages, America's workers didn't think they were getting a fair deal. Four-and-a-half million workers struck during the year. Major strikes at GM, U.S. Steel, and in the coal mines resulted in major gains for workers.

Prices rose rapidly because consumers had more money than ever after four years of wartime thrift, but there was little to spend their money on: American industry was slow to resume production of consumer goods. After so many years of austerity, people were in the mood to splurge. Vacations and leisure activities assumed new importance, assuring success of ventures like Bugsy Siegel's new Flamingo casino in Las Vegas and the newly formed National Basketball Association.

As the US military scaled back from 11 million to 1 million, birth rates rose 20 percent, starting the baby boom.

Overseas, relations between the United States and the Soviet Union degraded into suspicion and hostility

as Stalin closed the borders of what would become the Eastern Bloc, completely isolating eastern Europe from the West.

Justice was meted out to the surviving Nazi leaders at the conclusion of the Nuremburg war crimes trials. The most prominent Nazi to be tried, Hermann Goering, cheated the noose by biting into a cyanide capsule one hour before he was to hang.

The big news in science was the invention of the computer. At the University of Pennsylvania, the world's first electronic calculator, the Electrical Numerical Integrator and Calculator (ENIAC), was demonstrated. Not quite portable, the new machine used 18,000 vacuum tubes to perform 5,000 steps per second.

With its commitments to the war effort successfully completed, H-D eagerly resumed the business they knew best: the production of America's best motorcycles.

THE 1946 KNUCKLEHEAD

The OHV Big Twin model line for 1946 included three versions of each model, the high-compression 46EL and 46FL Special Sport Solos for $463.67 and $465, respectively, the medium-compression 46E and 46F twins at the same prices as the EL and FL, and the 46ES and 46FS twins with sidecar gearing, again at the same prices as the EL and FL. As before, the 61 models were only $1.33 cheaper than the 74 OHVs. All prices were the same as the previous year's, and the additional $4.08 ($2.04 per tire) surcharge was still levied on the 74 OHV models for their synthetic tires, raising the base price to $469.08. The cost of these tires was still built into the base price for the 61 models. For 1946, two standard colors were initially available: red or gray.

As in 1945, two option groups were offered. The Utility Solo Group included a front safety guard, steering damper, trip odometer, jiffy stand, 5.00x16-inch tires, and black rims, all for a cost of $14.50 (or $12 when fitted to sidecar or package truck motorcycles, on which the jiffy stand was omitted). The Special Solo Group included a front safety guard, steering damper, hydraulic shock absorber for the forks, jiffy stand, air cleaner, rear safety guard, trip odometer, mirror, 5.00x16 tires,

The 1941 clutch was much stronger, less prone to chatter, and cheaper to produce than the earlier clutch, and it would be used almost without change on all subsequent Harley-Davidson Big Twins into the early 1980s.

sheepskin saddle cover, solo windshield, and black rims, all for $55. See the discussion that follows for more information on option groups.

The early 1946 machines, built in late 1945 and early 1946, were only slightly dressier than their wartime siblings had been because chrome and aluminum were still in short supply. The main difference was that red paint was offered in addition to the wartime gray.

Other options became available as the year progressed. Black rubber grips became available in November 1945, according to the November 12, 1945, dealer news bulletin. Availability of foot pedal rubbers was announced in the January 21, 1946 news bulletin.

On February 5 and after, gray was dropped as a color option and was replaced by Skyway Blue, according to the news bulletin of that date.

The February 18 news bulletin heralded the return of aluminized paint, which meant that Police Silver was once again available for police models. Aluminized silver paint was probably used again on the tappet blocks and oil pumps after that date, replacing the white paint that had been used during the war. A supplement to the February 18 bulletin also listed new accessories and changes to the Special Solo Group. Added to the group were chrome fender tips, deluxe saddlebags, colored shift ball, and rubber pedal pads; the price was raised to $75. These new items were also available outside the group.

The factory seems to have experienced a shortage of four-speed transmissions, because the May 27 news bulletin announced that, beginning on that date, and without notice, an unspecified percentage of nonpolice orders would be shipped with the three-speed in order to maintain production.

Much later in the production run, such niceties as stainless steel for the fender trim and chrome for the pushrod tubes probably became available. The machines gradually began to look like civilian motorcycles again.

Even though many 1946 OHVs were wartime plain, they looked like sparkling jewels to motorcyclists who had been deprived of new machines for so long. But after the dressier bikes became available once again, the formerly sparkling jewels began to look as plain as they really were. Naturally enough, most of them were soon outfitted with the glossier parts. Original and restored machines with wartime finishes on their parts are almost never seen.

"Bull-Neck" Frame

Stability problems with the 5.00x16-inch tires had been largely solved when the neck angle was changed from twenty-eight degrees to twenty-nine degrees in 1941. Even so, H-D engineers introduced a revised frame for 1947 featuring a more massive neck forging with a 30-degree neck angle. The new forging is more massive overall, and the diameter of the neck is larger than the diameter of the neck cup, making less of the cup visible. Because of its stout construction, the new forging earned the nickname of "bull-neck." This new neck forging is correct for 1946 through mid-1947.

The thirty-degree neck angle did give an extra margin of stability and safety, at the cost of slower, heavier steering—but H-D's customers didn't seem to mind. By another degree, the OHV sportbike H-D had introduced in 1936 continued its evolution toward its destiny as a heavy, stable touring bike.

Mechanical Updates

After so many years with so few changes, the OHV Big Twin's design was in definite need of updating. Most of the updates were made as running changes during the production year.

In midyear, a new tab for affixing the spark control spiral to the frame was added to the lower tank mount on the left front downtube. The separate clamp for the coil was no longer used.

Early in the production run, the forks were given revised spring-rod-ball bushings and a ball-bushing retainer plate. After April 29, according to the October 21, 1946, dealer news bulletin, the inline forks were replaced by "offset" forks that are identical to the inline forks, except that the neck on the offset forks angled back so that it is behind the centerline of the rigid fork legs at the top of the forks. New handlebars were designed with a revised center section for use with offset springer forks. The center hole on the center section is offset to the rear of the two holes for the rigid fork legs. The offset forks and bars were also used in 1947.

About midway through production, the fenders were given wider braces. Still later, the fenders were once again drilled for the stainless-steel trim strips that became available after wartime restrictions were lifted. The updated fenders were also used in 1947.

The headlight mount was redesigned to have an integral top horn mount, and the mounts were used again in 1947.

In late 1946, the front rocker housing was slightly revised. The new housing is like the previous housing, except that the bottom surface was milled flat and the mold was revised to thicken the casting in the area around the intake pushrod hole. It was used again for 1947.

Finally, in late 1946, the clutch pedal was recontoured so that the heel pad was offset to the left by about ¼ inch. It was used again for 1947.

1946 Production

The war was won, the boys were coming home, and most prewar motorcycles were worn out because of the lack of spares during the wartime years. H-D was able to sell all the motorcycles they could find raw materials to build. According to the September 1946 *The Enthusiast*, "The demand for new Harley-Davidsons has been so overwhelming that we found it necessary to allot motorcycles to dealers on a quota basis." Despite shortages, production rose to 6,746 OHVs, higher than for any preceding year. Of this total, 2,098 were ELs, 244 were ESs, 3,986 were FLs, and 418 were FSs.

Clearly, the market was still there in postwar America for H-D's flagship Big Twin—all H-D had to do was figure out how to make enough to satisfy the demand.

The rocket-fin muffler introduced for 1941 helped modernize the look of the Knucklehead.

4
POSTWAR KNUCKLEHEADS

Optimism. That's the word that summed up the country's mood in 1947. The economy was booming again. Employment was down to 3.9 percent, and the GNP was rising at a rate of 11 percent. Farmers were raising bumper crops, yet prices stayed high. The only blight was an inflation rate of 8.4 percent, fueled by the

A premier collector bike today, this classic 1939 Knucklehead was just another entry in this endurance run held at Beaver Dam, Wisconsin, in 1941. Stuck in the mud, everyone along the route helped push to get it out. *Herbert Wagner Collection*

OPPOSITE: Indicative of an early customized Harley, this 1947 FL sports many features not found on a stock model. *Doug Mitchel*

housing shortage. The last real vestige of wartime shortages of consumer goods, sugar rationing, finally ended by midyear, and meat consumption rose to five nights a week for the average American family. Over a million former servicemen entered college on the GI Bill and prepared for a more prosperous future.

If anything, the mood was even more jubilant at the H-D factory in Milwaukee. After weathering the Great Depression, World War II, and the shortages and rationing that were the war's lingering legacy, the company was stronger than ever. And their OHV Big Twin, the flagship of the world's largest motorcycle fleet, was still the best and most technologically advanced American production motorcycle, eleven years after its introduction.

Harley's main rival, Indian, was still peddling flatheads, and was rapidly losing market share to H-D's OHV. Despite shortages of materials that had kept H-D from meeting demand, 1946 had been the best sales year ever for the OHV; more than six thousand were sold.

As the November 1946 issue of *The Enthusiast* admitted, "For quite some time, we have been rationing our motorcycles to dealers on a quota basis. . . . We are sorry, of course, that so many enthusiasts have experienced delays in getting their new Harley-Davidsons."As the 1947 models began rolling off the production line in the fall of 1946, the company was also busy preparing an extensively updated version of the OHV motor that would gain its own fame under the nickname

The shifter gate for 1947 was restyled to a boxier, more massive design than that used on the 1936–1946 Knuckleheads.

"Panhead." If the Knucklehead was so popular and so technologically far ahead of the competition, why expend the effort to replace it?

To answer the first part of the question, Indian wasn't the real competition anymore—that threat had been eclipsed by heightened expectations and new machines from overseas. When the Knucklehead was introduced, biplanes were still the norm in the US Army Air Corps. By war's end, even sleek, 400-mph monoplanes like the P-51 Mustang looked obsolete compared to the jet fighters that were just entering service. By early 1947, jets were the norm, and the even faster rocket-powered experimental planes represented the leading edge of engineering and speed.

At the same time, light, fast, sophisticated motorcycles were beginning to flood onto US shores from Great

Britain. The young and the reckless who had been the primary market for motorcycles—which in that era included thousands of discharged pilots, sailors, and soldiers who were looking for a new jag to replace the terrifying thrills of combat—were not going to be satisfied for long with Harley's old "biplane."

While H-D probably couldn't have guessed how thoroughly the middleweight British machines would come to dominate the US market in the next ten years, they didn't care: the testosterone-charged daredevil was no longer the company's intended customer. After all, these customers were fickle, likely to switch to the hottest new machine to come along, whatever the brand. For better or worse, H-D abandoned these riders to the British and staked the company's future on making their motorcycles appeal to a larger segment of society and on hooking their customers for life.

Turns out this was a great long-term strategy but a poor short-term tactic, because there were more performance-oriented customers waiting than H-D would have ever guessed. More than ten thousand British motorcycles were sold in 1946, and another fifteen thousand in 1947.

As we have already seen, H-D began trading performance for civility on the Knucklehead during its very first year, and, by 1947, the design of the bike had evolved so far away from its sportbike origins that there was no turning back. When H-D introduced their redesigned engine for 1948, it was one that would help carry the company further down the evolutionary path that led toward the big, reliable cruisers it still builds today.

In the meantime, H-D kept its corporate fingers crossed. Barring any unforeseen shortages or a fresh outbreak of war, 1947 looked to be the year the company would cash in.

IT'S A KNUCKLEHEAD WORLD, 1947

Tensions were building between the US and the Soviet Union—and between the US government and its few dissenting citizens. Bernard Baruch coined a chilling phrase when he implored: "Let us not be deceived. Today we are in the midst of a cold war. Our enemies are to be found abroad and at home."

Some prewar riders didn't make it back from World War II. One was Bud Waldman of Milwaukee, seen here on his first-year Knucklehead, 36EL1740, at the Kenosha, Wisconsin, TT races held in 1937. *Herbert Wagner Collection*

To stem the tide of Communism abroad, the United States embarked on its policy of "containing" the Soviets. As part of the containment strategy, President Truman requested $17 billion in aid to America's war-ravaged allies and enacted the Marshall Plan to rebuild Europe.

But who were "our enemies" at home? Like Kilroy was during the war, these enemies were everywhere, especially in government and in the movies. President Truman ordered FBI loyalty checks on federal employees to weed out "Socialists, Communists, and fellow travelers," and the House Un-American Activities Committee (HUAC) investigated the Communist infiltration of Hollywood. Instead of containment, suspected communists in Hollywood were "blacklisted."

The sport of motorcycling was given a black eye as a result of exaggerated publicity concerning a few instances of inebriated motorcyclists taking liberties in the town of Hollister, California, on July 4. The movie

This bagger probably would have won the "best-dressed machine" award at one of the AMA club events of the day. It was restored by Carman Brown.

The Wild One, starring Marlon Brando, was later based on the incident.

Television continued its takeover of the airwaves. The World Series (Dodgers versus Yankees) and a presidential speech (in which President Truman implored Americans to conserve food so that more could be sent to Europe) were each televised for the first time. Exciting

Among the EL's favored styling cues are the round air-intake bell, tombstone taillight, springer fork, and post-mounted pogo seat.
Doug Mitchel

A red 1947 EL parked in the snow in front of a tall evergreen. It's beginning to look a lot like Christmas! *Doug Mitchel*

Three riders toasting Bill Harley's great design masterpiece, the 1936 EL Knucklehead 61 OHV at Elkhart Lake in 1940. A little more than a year after Pearl Harbor, many of these same guys would be in the armed forces and the carefree, prewar party days would be over for the duration of the war. *Herbert Wagner Collection*

Winter riding was a popular pastime, and Harley-Davidson offered a full line of winter accessories and gear. This view shows a 45-inch Harley flathead on Pewaukee Lake near Milwaukee in 1933. *Herbert Wagner Collection*

new shows like *Howdy Doody* mesmerized the first of the baby boomers, and the Kraft Television Theater proved the marketing potential of the new medium as sales of Kraft cheese skyrocketed.

Strife between labor and industry continued. Telephone workers and coal miners struck and made major gains before unions were neutered by the provisions of the Employers Rights Act. Henry Ford, perhaps the staunchest opponent of unions, passed away on April 7.

Advancing science, a new "cure" for schizophrenia was announced: the prefrontal lobotomy. Edwin Land invented the Land camera. Admiral Richard Byrd explored Antarctica.

Aviation in this year really took off. Pan American World Airways began round-the-world service in the Lockheed Constellation *America*. The big aviation event occurred on October 14, when the laconic Capt. Charles E. Yeager—flying the world's most dangerous aircraft, despite having broken his ribs in a tumble from a horse— flew the Bell X-1 rocket-powered aircraft through the "sound barrier" over Muroc Air Force Base, becoming the first hero of the supersonic age.

Meanwhile, Jackie Robinson became the first African-American player to break the "color barrier" in the major leagues when he signed with the Brooklyn Dodgers. And H-D was poised to break through a barrier of its own, the twenty-thousand-sales barrier. Not since 1929, the year of the stock market crash that started the Great Depression, had sales of H-D civilian motorcycles surpassed this mark.

THE 1947 KNUCKLEHEADS

By 1947, the Knucklehead's major shortcomings had all been ironed out. Most of the changes to be made were limited to restyling, which would give the motorcycle a fresh, new postwar look.

The OHV Big Twin model line for 1947 included the high-compression 47EL and 47FL Special Sport Solos, the medium-compression 47E and 47F solo twins, and the 47ES and 47FS twins with sidecar gearing. The EL, E, and ES models were listed at a retail price of $590

This close-up of the forks shows the hydraulic shock absorber that first became optional in late 1945.

Note the shift knob, which is the "Saturn" type introduced in 1942, with the raised ring around its beltline.

(almost $130 more than in 1946); the FL, F, and FS models were listed at $605 ($145 more than in 1946). As the listing shows, retail prices had increased over 20 percent for 1947, mostly the result of the high prices H-D was forced to pay for aluminum, steel, rubber, and chrome; the easing of price controls and lingering scarcity were largely to blame. Other manufacturers were forced to raise their prices, too.

Putting the best possible face on the increase, H-D called it "moderate," and boasted in the November 1946 issue of *The Enthusiast* that, "It is only because of the foresight and judgment gained by long experience, plus advanced manufacturing methods, that prices have been kept down to their present level." All Harley models had to be ordered with one of the option groups, at additional cost. A four-speed transmission was standard,

but a three-speed transmission could be specified at the time of order for no additional cost. A special Police Combination with three-speed transmission and medium gearing was recommended for police work in the city or in service in congested traffic. Speedster handlebars could also be substituted for the standard bars for no extra cost.

Again for 1947, only two major option groups were offered for solo motorcycles, but for 1947, two versions of each were offered—with hydraulic shock absorber and without. The Utility Solo Group included a trip odometer, steering damper, hydraulic shock absorber, front safety guard, jiffy stand, chrome fender lamp, and 5.00x16-inch tires, all for $34 ($26.50 with ride control in place of the shock absorber). Sidecar and package truck machines were fitted with the Utility Group, which

This carburetor-off view shows how the oil is routed from the top of the gear-case cover to the rocker housings atop each head.

came in two versions and included the same items as the Utility Solo Group, minus the jiffy stand—all for $31.50 ($24 with ride control in place of the hydraulic shock absorber).

The only upgrade package offered for solo machines was the Special Solo Group. This group included a trip odometer, steering damper, hydraulic shock absorber, front safety guard, jiffy stand, rear safety guard, set of three foot pedal rubbers, colored shift ball, deluxe saddlebags, 5.00x16-inch tires, chrome fender light, chrome air cleaner, chrome headlamp, pair of chrome fender tips, chrome exhaust-pipe covers, chrome spotlights and fork bracket, and chrome parking lamps—all for $100 ($92.50 with ride control in place of the shock absorber).

The basic package for sidecar and package truck machines was the Utility Group, which included a

The new taillight introduced in 1947 was quickly dubbed the "tombstone" taillight because of its shape. It had an integral license plate frame, a top window to illuminate the license plate, and a red "Stimsonite" refracting rear lens. The chrome-plated rear lens retainer was optional; the standard retainer was painted black.

This nice 1947 FL is a top-of-the-line bike with almost every option, and even some extra chrome that wasn't available on a new machine, such as the exhaust pipes, muffler, and rear safety guard. The saddlebags are aftermarket bags designed to mount to the rear fender rack.

hydraulic shock absorber, safety guard, steering damper, front fender lamp, trip odometer, and 5.00x16-inch tires—all for $31.50 ($24 with ride control in place of the shock absorber).

The 1947 Knuckleheads were available in five standard colors: Brilliant Black, Skyway Blue, Flight Red, or Police Silver (police only).

Styling

For its last year, the Knucklehead was restyled to give it a more modern, postwar look. The centerpieces of the restyle—new tank emblem, tankshift gate, instrument panel, and restyled speedometer face—were clustered on the tank, but subtle styling changes stretched all the way back to the new taillight.

Instrument Panel

Perched atop the gas tanks was a new instrument panel that echoed the lines of the tank emblem. At the front, the instrument panel encircles the round speedometer dial, much like the front of the emblem encircles the red ball. And the rear of the instrument panel tapers gracefully before ending in a blunt chisel point, just as the emblem's banner does. The instrument panel is painted the main color of the tank.

The panel is fastened to the tank by a chrome-plated mounting bolt located just aft of the speedometer. Rather than using separate lenses for the two warning lights, the new dash has just one red lens, located just aft of the mounting bolt. The wide, rectangular, red lens covers the generator and oil warning lights, with the oil

ABOVE: Brown's 1947 Knucklehead carries the deluxe solo seat that was optional from 1947–1954. Whitewall tires were not available on a new machine from Harley-Davidson in 1947, but may have been available from the aftermarket.

BELOW: With all the items available in the Harley-Davidson accessory catalog and in the burgeoning aftermarket, the slim and elemental Knucklehead could be transformed into a long-distance hauler.

As Harley-Davidson ramped up production for the 1947 Model EL, company engineers were preparing a completely new Big Twin for the 1948 model year. *David Blattel*

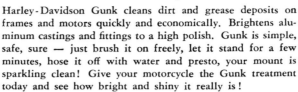

The commercial use of the motorcycle goes back to the origin of the device when doctors used them to make house calls. Later they were popular as delivery vehicles. The Gilmore Parcel Delivery service of Fond du Lac, Wisconsin, had a large fleet of sidecar package trucks in service before World War II. *Herbert Wagner Collection*

light on the right and the generator light on the left. Aft of the lens is the ignition switch. A hole for the police speedometer lock is on the panel's left side, and a slot for the tripmeter reset lever is on the right side. The new hole and slot covers are retained by clips rather than screws. Also for 1947, the gap between the lower edge of the instrument panel and the gas tank was sealed by a rubber molding.

Revised Gas Tanks

To accommodate the revised pieces attached to it, the gas tanks were updated with new mounts for the new emblems (and the stainless-steel strip mounts were deleted), a recessed mounting area on the left tank for the new shift gate, and reshaped dash-mount bases for the restyled dash. These new tanks are correct for 1947–1950.

"Tombstone" Taillight

At the rear, a new taillight was fitted to match the other, more angular styling cues introduced for 1947. Instead of tapering gracefully as the 1939–1946 "boattail" taillight did, the 1947 taillight was squared off at the rear. When viewed from the back, the taillight looks like a tall rectangle with a semicircle on top—a profile reminiscent of tombstones, hence its nickname.

The taillight body was die-cast zinc alloy. The front of the body's top surface has a cast-in lug, to which the

license plate bracket attaches. On the top of the body, just aft of the license plate bracket, a window with a frosted glass lens allows light from the tail lamp to shine through and illuminate the license plate. The tombstone-shaped red rear lens has a molded-in Stimsonite refractor pattern to diffuse the light. Separate gaskets are fitted around the inside and outside edge of the lens, and these are covered by a lens retainer that is fastened to the body by three screws. A drain hole on the body, below the lens, helps to purge moisture from the assembly. Another gasket is fitted between taillight body and fender, and the body is fastened to the fender by two screws.

Original taillights were fitted with a double-filament bulb of 21-3 candlepower. The standard tail lamp body, lens retainer, and license plate bracket are painted black, but these items may have been available in an optional chrome-plated finish later in the year, when chrome became more available. This taillight assembly was used on the 1947 Knucklehead and on all the later Panheads through 1954.

More Chrome and Cadmium Plating

"We are doing everything within our power to supply more chrome and there is more of it on our 1947 H-Ds than there has been for a long time," boasted the September 1946 issue of *The Enthusiast*. And the magazine wasn't lying. Chrome for plating was more available than it had been since before the war, so the switch back to shiny finishes on the parts that had begun in 1946 was essentially completed by the start of the 1947 season.

Once again, the handlebar switches, ignition-switch cover, horn cover, front fender light, instrument-cover mounting bolt, gas shut-off knob, gas caps, speedometer bezel, headlamp ring, and many other parts were chrome plated on the basic motorcycle, and chrome-plated

Another view of the 1947 Knucklehead restored by Elmer Ehnes.

optional accessories were offered, including front and rear fender tips, air-cleaner cover, headlamp, exhaust-pipe covers, and parking lamps.

Similarly, cadmium-plated parts were used in many of the same places as on the prewar bikes: kickstarter tube and end pieces, timer cover, seat-post tube, spoke nipples, light switch knob for the speedometer, and other small parts. Aluminized paint was also widely available once again, so the oil pump body and tappet blocks were once again painted silver. Wartime's ugly duckling could return to its role as peacetime's swan.

OPPOSITE: To allow the reversal of shift pattern (with first being the rearmost shifter position rather than the frontmost) without redesigning the shift drum or transmission, the shifter arm on the transmission was rotated 180 degrees so it points down, behind the primary cover.

Harley-Davidson offered both flathead or Knucklehead models for police use, but it was the Model FL, the larger-displacement version of the Knucklehead, that was most preferred by law-enforcement officers. *David Blattel*

Mel Krueger crashes a board wall at the Wausau Motorcycle Rodeo in 1936. Daredevil events like this one were once popular entertainment at motorcycle gatherings. *Herbert Wagner Collection*

Sunglasses go well with a 1961 OHV. *Herbert Wagner Collection*

Note how the rod from the tank shifter angles down behind the primary cover to attach to the arm. The patent decal shown on the coil should be on the left side of the oil tank. No decal is used on the right side.

New Neck Forging

Late in the 1947 production year, the frame's steering-head forging was given another update. The bull-neck forging that had been introduced in 1946 was replaced by a much slimmer forging. The neck of the new forging is about the same diameter on its upper and lower edges as the neck cups, but tapers to a much smaller diameter in the center section of the neck. This new neck forging was used only for late 1947.

Engine

Mechanical modifications for 1947 consisted of subtle refinements rather than radical changes. The 1947 tappet assemblies were fitted with an updated roller with needle bearings (replacing the roller bushing used from 1936–1946)

for smoother operation and longer wear. Each new tappet-roller assembly consists of a roller, a roller race, a roller axle pin, and twenty-five needle rollers. The new rollers were used again on the tappets for the 1948 Panhead motor.

The other notable engine update for the year was made to the ignition-timer assembly. On the 1936–1946 timers, the cable from the advance spiral on the handlebar is attached to a post on the timer strap, which clamped around the timer's base. For 1947, a new base was fitted. The new timer base has an adjustable post sticking straight to the side, to which the cable is attached, providing a more direct, simpler connection. The timer housing was revised with a $^{13}/_{16}$-inch notch on its top rim. The new post on the timer base protrudes out to the side of the timer assembly through the slot.

This 1947 Knucklehead has the "bull-neck" frame introduced in mid-1946 and used through most of 1947 production. Note how heavy the casting is around the lower cup for the steering-head bearing.

The slot allows clearance for the post to slide clockwise (retard) or counterclockwise (advance), and the slot's edges serve as the advance and retard stops. This style of advance mechanism was also carried over to the Panhead in 1948.

As part of the switch to the new timer assembly, a new cutout relay base was fitted. Relay bases since 1936 had an integral slot that served as the advance and retard stops for the pre-1947 timer assembly. The new relay base for 1947 lacks the slot. A redesigned bracket was used to fix the control coil in place.

1947 Production

As the company had hoped, 1947 was the best year for civilian sales since 1929—despite the substantial increase in price. H-D's records suggest that it sold 20,115 motorcycles in 1947. Of this total, 11,348 were Knuckleheads, including 4,117 ELs, 237 ESs, 6,893 FLs, and 401 FSs.

While sales of 11,000 Knuckleheads in a single year may not seem significant, comparison with sales figures from other years shows just how important the OHV Big Twin had become to the company. In its first year—1936—only 1,700–2,000 Knuckleheads were built, representing about 20 percent of H-D's motorcycle production. In its final year, 1947, Knuckleheads accounted for over half of H-D's sales. In its first four production years, 1936–1939, only about 9,300 Knuckleheads were built, almost 2,000 fewer than were sold in 1947 alone. In fact, almost one-third of all Knuckleheads ever built were built in 1947 alone. Even so, demand had not been met. What had once been a temperamental hot rod for the devil-may-care few had become a workaday mount for motorcycling's equivalent of "the masses."

THE FUTURE

The fall of 1947 brought the end of the Knucklehead—but also a new beginning for H-D. The November 1947 issue of *The Enthusiast* announced the "biggest motorcycle story of the year": the new OHV models that would carry the company into the future.

The big story? An updated top end for the OHV engine, consisting of aluminum cylinder heads, hydraulic valve

TWO-TONE CLOTH HELMET....1.95

BREECHES.............6.95-9.95-11.75

SET OF PADS......................12.50

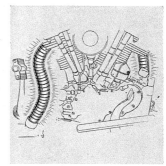

CHROME STACKS...........2.30-2.60

CHAIN GREASE..........................20

SADDLE BAGS.................29.95 pr.

BOOTS, C and D width........18.95

MEN'S JACKE1 33.00 LADIES' 24.90

CHROME CROSS BAR.............5.70

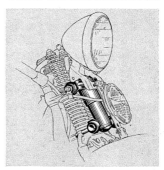

SHOCK ABSORBER................16.00

BUDDY SEAT......................29.75

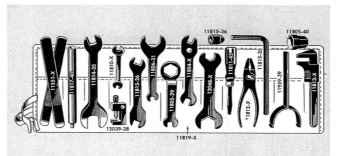

TOOL KIT.......................8.50

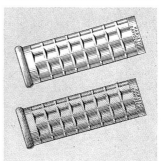

COLORED PLASTIC GRIPS........1.50

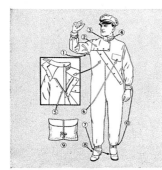

RAINSUIT................................16.95

GUNK COMPOUND M.........35 pt.

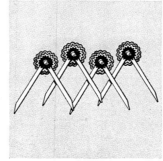

ROSETTES................................1.50

FRONTIER PANTS....................8.75

In front of Bill Knuth's H-D shop in Milwaukee, Wisconsin, 1949. *Herbert Wagner Collection*

You didn't have to be an outlaw to ride a motorcycle in the early days, but it helped. *Herbert Wagner Collection*

The Knucklehead: perhaps the most iconic profile in motorcycling.

lifters, redesigned cylinders with internal oil feed and return lines to and from the heads, and a chrome-plated, stamped-steel "pan" cover that completely enclosed the rockers and valves of each head. These updates made the motor smoother, quieter, more oil tight, cooler running, and more maintenance free—but not much lighter or more powerful.

Other than the top end, little else was changed for 1948. Even the styling was almost exactly the same as on the 1947 OHV. The changes that turned the Knucklehead into the Panhead were evolutionary, not revolutionary like those that turned H-D's old flathead into the 61 OHV in 1936. Even so, the new model was even more popular than the old, and 12,924 were sold.

The evolution continued in the years that followed. For 1949, hydraulic forks were introduced, giving rise to the first official H-D name for the OHV Big Twin: Hydra-Glide. During the early 1950s, the motor was gradually

This 1947 Knucklehead has the late 1947 frame with the much slimmer steering-head casting.

The Knucklehead—lean and mean on the left and baggerized on the right.

In the twenty-first century, it's easy to fall into the trap of looking at Knuckleheads as museum pieces, but they were built to be ridden and built to last. Here is the man who was likely the oldest living Harley rider in Milwaukee when this photo was taken in the mid-1990s. His name is Valentino "Vick" Domowicz, and this is his unrestored 1947 Knucklehead.

ABOVE: At the time, Domowicz was ninety-two and had been invited to the Juneau Avenue factory to meet Willie G. Davidson.

BELOW: I followed him to the factory, and Domowicz rode his Knucklehead with skill and gusto.

In overall looks, the Knucklehead didn't really change all that much from 1936 to 1947. Inside, the later Knuckles were vastly improved machines.

updated, the styling was changed slightly, and a foot-operated shifter and hand-operated clutch was introduced. In 1958, rear suspension was added, giving rise to the second official H-D name for the Big Twin: Duo-Glide. In the late 1950s and early 1960s, the British invasion waned, and H-D was forced to weather a new invasion, this time by the Japanese. H-D stayed on course, however, and their Panhead continued to evolve into a larger, heavier, touring-oriented machine. In 1965, electric starting was added for the Panhead's final year, sparking the third official H-D name for the Big Twin: Electra Glide.

In the beginning, the Panhead still was a fairly trim machine that many riders proved was capable of winning on the tracks, on the hills, and in the swamps of America. By the end, it weighed over seven hundred pounds in stripped form and more than eight hundred pounds once it was outfitted with fiberglass saddlebags,

windshield, dual exhaust, and all the chrome bits that were in fashion. In short, it had become the archetypal American touring machine.

For 1966, the Electra Glide was given a new motor featuring yet another redesign of the top end. It, too, was smoother, quieter, more oil tight, cooler running, and more maintenance free than its predecessor—but not much lighter or more powerful. And it, too, was eventually given a nickname: Shovelhead. Over time, many new features were introduced on the Electra Glide, including an alternator, disc brakes, and a real fairing. Then the chopper craze was given official sanction when H-D devolved the Electra Glide into a series of more elemental customs that gave variety to the lineup and appealed to new customers.

In 1984 came the V2 Evolution engine, the first true fulfillment of the promise made in 1936. The new engine was lightweight and as reliable and as maintenance free

Near Holy Hill outside of Milwaukee, Wisconsin, 1950. *Herbert Wagner Collection*

as the best of its competitors. When combined with restyled and updated chassis in new models, such as the Softail and FLHT, the Evolution engine finally gave H-D's Big Twin true mass-market appeal. As a result, by the early 1990s, the once-ailing Milwaukee firm would again achieve the same dominance in the American marketplace that they had enjoyed at the end of 1947.

But after eighty years of change, little really had. From Knucklehead, to Panhead, to Shovelhead, to Evo, to Twin Cam, to Rushmore, the basics of the 1936 OHV engine that had made it so appealing remained. In fact, maybe we're all being a bit myopic by encouraging the continued use of such distinctions.

The truth is, the Knucklehead was never really replaced by the Panhead—or by any of the others, for that matter. To H-D and to the enthusiasts of the day, there were no Knuckleheads or Panheads, only 61 or 74 OHVs. Later came the official names, such as those already mentioned and a whole slew of later ones—Super

Glide, Low Rider, Tour Glide, Softail—on and on. In fact, it wasn't until the V2 Evolution engine was introduced in 1984 that H-D even gave an official name to any of their OHV Big Twin engines. The switch from Knucklehead to Panhead that today seems such a definitive dividing point in H-D history was barely noticed by most riders—and it wasn't accompanied by a name.

As a result, somewhere along the way, enthusiasts found it convenient to coin names to distinguish between the variations on the OHV Big Twin motor. And the names are useful, in some ways. But let's not let them disguise the fact that what began with the 1936 61 continues today. The 61-cubic-inch 1936 overhead-valve V-twin has far more similarities to the 110-cubic-inch Twin Cooled Twin Cam (the Motor Company's names are now coined by marketing types rather than riders themselves, so they tend to be a bit clunky) powering today's $40,000 CVO Road Glide Ultra than differences. And that is the Knucklehead's greatest legacy.

INDEX